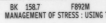

Management of Stress

David R. Frew

MANAGEMENT OF STRESS

Using TM at Work

Nelson-Hall nh Chicago

Library of Congress Cataloging in Publication Data

Frew, David R.
  Management of stress.

  Includes index.
  1. Work—Psychological aspects. 2. Stress
(Psychology) 3. Transcendental meditation.
4. Personnel management. I. Title.
HF5548.8.F745   158.7   76-18164
ISBN 0-88229-254-4

Copyright © 1977 by David R. Frew

Manufactured in the United States of America

to my family:

Mary Ann
Kristin, David, Cheryl

Contents

Preface

I suppose that anyone who writes a book must feel strongly about the potential value of his or her work. But in this particular case, I can't help feeling that my study of stress at work may point the way toward many of the root problems of our Western culture. Since my first job I have been questioning the structure of our work systems and their impact upon both the individual and his family. My formal study of the organizational sciences has reaffirmed my original notion that the job and the career have much more to do with "who we are" than many of us have recognized. And yet we continue to live in a very confused and random work-oriented society where there is seemingly little attention placed upon the feelings of the individual at his job. And this may be a primary source of difficulty for many members of our society.

The fundamental purpose of this book is to contribute to the quality of life of those persons who might be exposed to it. It has long been my contention that an improved understanding of work, work structure, and the delicate interrelationship between work and nonwork activities, holds great promise for improving both job and leisure satisfaction. It has been my experience that the more we seem to understand what is happening to us and why we feel the way we do, the better we are able to cope with our situations. So the chapters which follow attempt to paint a comprehensive picture of work, from the perspective of the individual employee. The focus is not placed upon the factory worker, or upon the executive, but rather upon the stresses and strains of earning a living—which would appear to affect both of them. The unique characteristic of the book is that it isolates stress as the major source of work-related difficulties, both at the job and at home. The highly stressed individual is inefficient at work, and at the same time unable to develop a satisfactory personal life.

This book *Management of Stress*, is not unique from the standpoint of any individual science or profession, since the theories and the research knowledge which comprise the core of the book have existed within their respective fields for some time. Perhaps the real contribution herein lies in the integration of several diverse literatures for the study of management process. Interdisciplinary approaches such as this one may, indeed, hold the answers to a number of troublesome problems.

It is also my hope that this book might reach a rather large and diverse audience. First and foremost, I feel that practicing managers or supervisors might find it to be a useful addition to their business libraries. *Management of Stress* might help them, not only to make their own working experience better, but to improve the quality of life for both their subordinates and their colleagues. Secondly, I would think that the book might help to produce some interesting insights for both students and professors of either management or organizational behavior. However, the most important audience for *Management of Stress* is the working person. It is he or she who might use the information herein to effect positive changes in his or her life.

Before moving on to the book, I feel compelled to take the time to acknowledge some of the people who have helped to make this project possible.

The most important single person in both the theoretical

and empirical developments of the project was, undoubtedly, my wife Mary Ann Frew. It was Mary Ann who first introduced me not only to the notion of meditation and stress release, but to the relationship between stress and my own field of organizational behavior. And then it was Mary Ann who encouraged my progress with the book, did most of the editing, and worked double duty by "covering for me" at home while I was doing the research. So to her and my children, Kristin, David, and Cheryl, I owe my appreciation.

I also owe a great debt to Dr. Michael Ferrari, Dr. Anant Negandhi, Dr. Robert Smith, Dr. Arlyn Melcher, and Dr. Albert Heinlein, who helped me to gain many insights into organizational behavior. Their contributions to the doctoral program in organization and administration at Kent State University have helped more than a few aspiring behavioral scientists. It has also been my good fortune to work with a number of very supportive people here at Gannon College. And to these colleagues—in particular Ronald Volpe, David Eichelsdorfer, William Latimer, and Dr. Joseph Scottino—I owe my continuing thanks for providing a work atmosphere conducive to research.

A number of graduate students who worked as my research assistants during the three years of work that went into this book also deserve some mention at this time. So to John Copple, Nick Ryback, and Craig Cunningham, who each contributed to the research, I express my sincere thanks. Special thanks to Jo Ann Walker, who labored through most of the rough draft work, and also typed much of the final manuscript.

Finally three other contributors deserve special mention: John W. O'Sullivan Gould, my current research assistant who made every imaginable contribution to the project including library research, data gathering, typing, and editing; Walter Wunch, who assisted me in gathering much of the data; and Thomas Leonardi, my good friend, who provided a good deal of psychological support and counsel during the project.

Introduction

I was privileged recently to work with Harold Bloomfield, a young psychiatrist from Yale, who has been doing research on the subject of stress from both the physiological and the psychiatric perspectives. His work has both solidified and magnified the importance of the study of stress at work which is the topic of this book. Dr. Bloomfield and other medical researchers have concluded that stress is our nation's number one health problem, and that many of the predominant illnesses such as heart disease, hypertension, alcoholism, and the abuse of prescription drugs are simply symptoms of this larger stress-oriented disorder.

Obviously, the purpose of this book is not to expound upon the health-care problems of the times. And yet it is clear to anyone who is paying attention to the world of work that Dr. Bloomfield's observations are well worth more than just a cursory observation. Many of us find ourselves to be working in highly stressed job environments; if not constantly, at least from time to time. We see the effects of work-orientated stress upon our colleagues—the hypertension, the ulcers, and the anxiety! But how does all of this affect each one of us? Can we hope to escape the effects of stress?

This is a book about stress. In the pages which follow we will explore some very fundamental questions. What is stress? Where does it come from? How is stress related to our jobs? Can good management practice help to avert stress? How can a person deal with stress? Does reduced stress affect job performance? The answers to these questions are not merely important to us. They are vital for survival in our increasingly complex work environments.

Man the Worker

Man is a unique creature. His life proceeds as a series of highly specialized, complicated, and interrelated activities. Most workers spend time working in their homes, and time with their families. Perhaps the complex problem of studying work behavior is that it overlaps all of the other aspects of life, and it overlaps them in several different ways.

First, most of us are not independently wealthy. Therefore to continue such enjoyable activities as eating and staying warm we usually must depend upon a source of employment for financial support. Secondly, we tend to choose our friends, our neighborhoods, and our leisure activities in terms of both our work status and our working schedule. Finally, our family structure is, many times, dictated by our jobs. For example, when both husband and wife work a common shift, children are apt to see less of their parents. If the husband and wife work different shifts, they must surely see considerably less of each other.

Another fundamental but important aspect of our working careers is the incredibly large percentage of time and productive energy which is almost always devoted to the job. If we focus upon the typical eight-to-five job, for example, it would seem that a person simply works eight hours a day. In terms of mathematics that is 33 percent of our time on a typical working day. But using a more realistic approach, what happens if we add up things like travel to and from work, lunch hours, preparation to go to work and time for unwinding? Moreover, what would happen if these were calculated as a percentage of hours awake rather than total hours? For example:

Preparation for work		30 min.
Travel to work		30 min.
Job time	8 hrs.	
Lunch time	1 hr.	
Travel home		30 min.
Unwinding time		30 min.

Total work-related time 11 hours
Percentage of total hours awake 69%
(rather than working hours)

Using these estimates, it soon becomes quite apparent that a typical working person spends close to 70 percent of his time awake either working or engaged in work-related activities. This analysis assumes an eight-to-five job. Naturally, as the job begins to incorporate such things as overtime, homework, and evening meetings, that percentage increases dramatically.

It is not quite clear why persons immerse themselves so deeply in their work, but research has suggested that the reasons go well byond the simple act of earning a living. It is clear that the executive, for example, with his countless hours of casual overtime is fulfilling needs for something well beyond dollars and cents.

The Drive to Do Well

Another notion which underlies this book is that we all want to do a good job! Now many of us would reject this principle on the basis of some of our experiences which might possibly suggest the opposite. After all, who has not seen several examples of persons who just do bad jobs? But why do they do these bad jobs? In my own experiences I can't think of a single example of a person who leaves his house in the morning, and says to his wife and children, "Well good-by, I'm off to do a lousy job today." When did you ever encounter a person who bragged about doing a bad job? The typical person integrates what he does at work with who he is. He somehow identifies himself with his activity and defines his role in life accordingly. How often is the ordinary introduction to a new person accompanied by a volley of "what do you do for a living?" questions? "This is Fred Smith, he is an engineer at Acme."

So since we all want to feel that we are important and useful people, and that others regard us that way, it is most normal to want to do well in our occupation. Thus, when a person does a bad job, the fault may in fact lie within the job environment or the management, rather than with the person who is doing the work.

Work and Stress

Since our identities are so strongly connected with what we do, our jobs become a major source of either satisfaction or dissatisfaction, and this feeling, either positive or negative, pours over into our personal lives. The net result is a very complicated and interconnected "work-non-work existence" in which each component of our lives directly influences the other. There is no simple dividing line between work and play. When we play we find that we think about and discuss our work; and when we work we usually find ourselves doing the opposite.

Thus stresses which result from our jobs overflow into our family and personal lives. They affect wives, children, Boy Scouts, Little Leagues, stamp collections, and every other leisure activity.

A colleague of mine who works in a people-oriented profession as a counselor once told me that for about a year he would come home each Tuesday night after work, yell at his children, have a fight with his wife, eat dinner, sit down, and fall asleep. It was only after several months of this behavior that he and his wife caught on to the fact that something very unique was happening at work on Tuesdays which caused him to become very highly stressed. His is one of hundreds of thousands of examples of how a job can have an impact upon one's entire life.

Another classic example is the keyed-up executive who rushes to the golf course so that he can hit golf balls badly. He stews about his job while he golfs, and he stews about his golf while he works. His prospects for playing a good game of golf or working at his full creative potential are not quite as good as his prospects for a heart attack!

The Price of Stress

The cost of stress is twofold. The first is inefficiency at work, which can be translated either in terms of the individual or the company. A highly stressed individual simply cannot work effectively at a creative position or, for that matter, at a noncreative position. This means that particularly for those who work as managers or administrators, or whose occupations demand a great deal of interaction with people, or whose jobs require creative and intuitive capacity, stress robs the ability to be productive. For the company it follows that highly stressed people hinder organizational efforts to attain goals.

The second cost of stress is paid in terms of our personal lives. Here stress causes a reduction in the quality of interpersonal relationships with our families and friends. Stress makes us tired, lifeless, and disinterested in things that are happening. It reduces us to a nation of TV watchers who pass out from stress overdoses night after night in front of the electronic box. Stress reduces our enjoyment of and capacities for our hobbies and activities. Our golf, swimming, and tennis become less frequent and less enjoyable.

And to fulfill the stress syndrome, many of us turn to overeating, drinking the extra Manhattan, or taking tranquilizers to try to combat the mounting feelings of despair. These reactions further decrease our creative capacity, and also increase the level of stress so that we become even less effective than we were.

The Purpose of the Book

I am writing this book in the hope that it might help

persons recognize and deal with stress. More than any other single factor, I believe that stress, and particularly work related stress, can erode the very quality of life. Stress doesn't simply make us ineffective at our jobs since there is no neat and simple way of separating our jobs from ourselves. Neither does it affect any other single dimension of our existence. The "stress syndrome" is both insidious and powerful. As we grow in terms of responsibility as well as age, our complex technical culture increasingly surrounds us with stressors. In fact it is clear that all of us will be subjected to an increasing array of stress-producing agents as time goes on.

As my research draws me further into this area I think that I am quickly learning to physically and behaviorally recognize the impacts of stress on the people around me. There is an objective stress syndrome which manifests itself in both the appearance and the behavior of those who are affected. People who are highly stressed look stressed. They exhibit the physiology and the behavior of stress sickness.

And yet I can also report, quite happily, that many persons seem to emerge from super-stress situations without the scars of adaptation. They seem to be happier, more productive, and more fulfilled than most of the rest of us. They are healthy, enthusiastic, and vigorous about life. How is it that these select few can live in the same world with the rest of us and yet avoid the harassment of their complex environment?

It is my firm belief that the impact of stress can be significantly reduced by persons who will thoughtfully approach the question of stress management. Moreover this decision to actively address oneself to the issue of stress is perhaps the single most important step that one can take to expand the quality of his or her life. The management of stress can improve every aspect of our existence. And while the basic thrust of this book will be to study the impact of work stress on the worker and conversely the impact of stress reduction upon work, the benefits of stress reduction must surely overflow into our personal lives. Simply stated, we do a better job at work, and then we feel better when we go home. How often have we witnessed this phenomenon in reverse: a bad day at the office followed by a fight with the spouse or an impatience with our children.

Stress causes a vicious cycle. We begin (starting in the middle of an endless cycle) by having a mediocre or worse day at the job. We stew about work on the way home and then proceed to take out our frustrations and anxieties on our family or friends. Following an unsatisfactory evening with the family we stew all the way to work and begin another bad day, perhaps even worse than the one before.

Where does this all end? How can each of us stop this vicious stress cycle? Learning to recognize and deal with stress is the only method for reducing the impact that our harried environments have upon us. We must convince ourselves of the existence of stressors within our own personal environment and determine a course of action for insulating ourselves. There are many effective methods for dealing with stress not the least important of which is simply the recognition of the phenomenon and its impact upon us. This management of stress can then improve every single aspect of our lives. Just as stress can cause a vicious cycle effect, proper stress management can lead to the opposite phenomenon. Our jobs become enjoyable, positive experiences which enrich our lives rather than providing a source of tension. Our family life takes on a new level of quality, since we have more energy and a better self to offer to our spouses and to our children. Our leisure time becomes leisure—not a stress-filled extension of our jobs.

The Organization of the Book

The pages which follow include three major sections. First is *Management, Stress, and the Worker*. The chapters within this section are oriented toward describing the existence of stress and the relationship between stress and the work environment. This introduction proposes a general view of man as increasingly trapped within a maze of stress, and suggests the relationship between work and one's personal life. The first chapter paints a dramatic picture of the kinds of changes which have continued to develop within work organizations. This will serve to introduce the problems which face both managers and workers within contemporary organizations. Chapter 2 presents a systematic, if not scientific, view of current management technology. What do we now know about the process of management—how are people organized, motivated and led? It is from this platform of managerial competence that we can begin to understand and deal with stress. Finally, the third chapter itemizes and describes the work-related factors which cause stress.

The next major section of the book is entitled, *The Impact of Stress*. Here both the psychological and physiological aspects of stress will be presented along with a systematic view of the relationship between stress and productivity. Chapter 4, The Psychophysiology of Stress, contains an overview of the scientific literature on stress. What is stress? Where does it come from? Specifically, what does it do to us? Many of the answers to these questions are quite shocking! The fifth chapter, The Science of Creative Intelligence, will attempt to integrate the physiologist's understanding of stress with the physician's regard for health, the philosopher's concern for human development, and the manager's drive for efficiency. How can stress reduction improve each of us in terms of our self-awareness, our self-concepts, our relationships with others, and our productivity?

Section three, *Productivity and Stress*, deals specifically with the impact of one particular approach to stress reduction. Transcendental Meditation, which is introduced and explained in general terms within Chapter 5, is investigated in terms of its impact at work. Chapter 6 asks, "What is the effect of reduced stress (as a result of meditation) upon work-related behavior? What happens to turnover, productivity, interpersonal relationships, ambition, and job satisfaction as a result of reduced stress?" While Chapter 6 deals with stress reduction from the individual perspective, Chapter 7 focuses upon the impact of stress reduction at the organizational level. The eighth chapter presents a number of additional stress reducing techniques which can be used in combination with or in place of TM by individuals who want to reduce their levels of stress.

The ninth and concluding chapter includes forward-looking strategies and prescriptions for organizational men of the year 2000. How can we insulate ourselves against Alvin Tofler's future shock?

While I remain more than just a little bit concerned about the whole stress picture for our society in general and more particularly for those of us who work for a living, I continue to be encouraged by the research that I see. There is every reason to believe that the person who will address himself to the problem of stress and make positive steps toward dealing with his own situation can significantly improve the overall quality of his life. The management of stress which will be presented in the pages that follow, provides some very exciting and promising prospects for all of us!

part 1
Management, Stress, and the Worker

chapter 1

The Evolution of Organized Society

Perhaps the most important step toward an improved understanding of work and stress, is a clear view of the impact of contemporary organizations upon people. Thus this chapter will deal with organization, the phenomenon. What is it? Where did it come from? How does it affect those of us who work within its clutches? And how did it get to be the way that it is?

The Old Days

Life styles have changed so drastically within the past few decades that most of us could not begin to understand the extent or intensity, of the evolution of work patterns. Looking at what might be viewed by historians as a rather short time span, these patterns of work have been altered so dramatically that if one of us were to be transported by a magic time

1

machine to the world of a hundred years ago, we would surely be aliens in a strange culture.

But, one of the attributes of this change which has made it palatable is the fact that it proceeds gradually rather than all at once. Thus it is possible for a person to immerse himself in life and become oblivious to the great movement of the world about him. It is like the small boat drifting along a river. Unless its captain glances toward shore from time to time, he has little understanding of his motion. But the gradualness of this change which engulfs and encases each of us also has a rather bad effect. Unless we are careful to tune into the process of change itself, we risk the great danger of losing touch with the real world; the river bank in our previous example.

Perhaps the most important arena of change which affects the life styles of all people, lies within the world of work. A century ago, people just did not proceed in the ways which are commonly accepted today. The five-day, forty-hour workweek was not the norm! For our great-great-grandfathers, the basic task was essentially the same as ours—to earn a living for themselves and for their families. But the approach was very different. Instead of piling into commuter trains or zipping through traffic en route to the office or factory, the work of our great-great-grandfathers was much more individualistic. People of that generation were much more likely to be involved in either agrarian or craft-oriented work. They grew food or raised stock. They worked at crafts. In any case they were much more closely tied to the ultimate ends of their work than most of us could ever hope to be—i.e. growing corn is more easily connected to eating than being an accountant.

The Transition

So how did we do it? How did we make the transition from that placid preindustrial state to the action-packed world where we now live? The answer is organization. Yes, that's correct. The organization of large groups of people into systematic goal-seeking units has been responsible for both the good and bad effects of industrialization. Or in other words, one of the fundamental differences between our lives and those of our great-great-grandfathers, lies in the fact that we work for superlarge organizations. Rather than scratching the soil for our food and felling trees to create shelter, we report to General Motors, or General Electric, or IBM, and we trade our services for our needs.

Like most change, however, this transition did not take place overnight. It grew slowly, year by year. But how did it happen, and why? The answers to these questions will provide the first clues for understanding some of the major sources of stress!

The Search for an Approach

Evidently the first men who stepped off into the industrial revolution were making a kind of instant transition from artisans to industrialists. In short, they were transferring a skill, which they themselves had developed, into an assembly-line process. To do this they needed to train many different persons to accomplish component parts of their respective trades. The basic question at the time was one of organization. How were large numbers of people to be organized into an effective structure for purposes of goal accomplishment?

Now if I were to ask one of my classes to draw up a design for the best possible gasoline engine, they would use a modeling approach. That means that instead of starting from scratch they would probably begin with an analysis of available gasoline-engine designs. They could, for example, run to the nearest parking lot and open hoods in search of the best possible existing engine. This approach is a normal, sensible, and efficient way to solve a unique problem. And this is the approach utilized by the first industrialists. They looked for and seized the most practical and successful existing answers to the problem of how to organize.

And so it was that two very unlikely and extraordinary organizational models became the prototypes for management: Napoleon's army and the Roman Catholic Church.[1] Both of these had existed successfully, accomplished goals, and, more

importantly, left a written record of their deeds. Early practitioners, as well as students of the art of management, were able
to use these sources for advice and counsel as they planned
their own enterprises. They were able to avoid the problems
which were encountered and solved by the designers of these
first prototype organizations.

Organizational Skeletons from the Past

Incredible as it may seem, the influence that the early
industrial revolution had upon organizational styles continues
to exist in today's work world. In fact, to merely say that it lives
may, to a large extent, be a gross understatement. This strong
influence from the turn-of-the century management approach
which we might call "classical management" can be traced
from early influences such as Napoleon, the Catholic Church,
and Max Weber,[2] through the writings of the first management
theorists such as Frederick Taylor[3] and Henry Fayol,[4] to the
ongoing structures of many current major corporations.

To exemplify this point, the Gannon College Graduate
School of Business, my employer, hosts a lecture series which
usually emphasizes successful executives and their practical
experience. One lecturer, the operating manager of a large
division of a major corporation, showed up with his copy of
the company's official management guide: the rule book for
upper-level administrators. This book could have been a
carbon copy of the writings of classical theorists.

Let us typify this approach which has dominated the
management thinking of organizations for the past century. It
has been called many things: Theory X, autocratic, Taylorism,
authoritarian, manipulative, bureaucratic, or traditional. In
essence, its doctrine is to organize people in a kind of World
War II army arrangement with division of labor, hierarchy,
authority, responsibility and fixed chains of command.

A Revolution

Sometime during the late 1930s or early 1940s, however,
the peaceful and systematic progress of classical management
theory was shattered by the impact of the Hawthorne Studies.[5]

A group of traditionally oriented researchers who were looking at ways to increase productivity made the astute discovery that by simply paying attention to employees, listening to their problems, and showing an interest in them as people, productivity could be greatly increased. These gains in productivity were shown to be far greater than any gains resulting from the technical adjustments which were part of their studies.

Thus a new management approach was born. And *human relations* became the key word for this alternative style. While the human relations teachings did not have the massive impact of the classical school, the fifties and sixties saw many managers reading and discussing human relations theory.

The working manager who turned to the literature for advice during the sixties would undoubtedly have faced a tremendous conflict. In one corner was the assembled classical theorists with their history of success dating back to the turn of the century. In the other corner was a massive group of contemporary human-relations-oriented people, such as McGregor,[6] Hertzberg,[7] Argyris,[8] and Likert,[9] who pointed to recent trends, studies, and a changing world. And as the theorists fought on, the people who worked in the real world could do little more than watch as they attended to their everyday jobs as managers. Management theory was providing little or no help for management practice.

A Visionary

But the sixties also bought some new approaches to management. And one of these, systems theory, began to tie together the loose ends of management. Perhaps the champion of the new approach was Warren Bennis[10] whose theories focused upon the changing patterns of work. He suggested that the past few decades had brought incredible levels of technical change. The work world of 1960 was much more complex than the corresponding work world of the fifties, and this change was proceeding at a geometric rate.

Bennis' work, which was recently amplified by Alvin Toffler[11] in his popular *Future Shock*, indicated that since the industrial revolution our jobs have changed radically. While

work was once dominated by simple and easily understood
jobs, such as running a punch press or a drill press, the world
of the 1970s is typified by a very different kind of job. Today's
work culture has evolved into a much more complex system.
Individual jobs are much more complex and technically
demanding. And at the same time, the rate of technical
obsolescence is increasing so that most jobs either change in
character or disappear within a relatively short time.

By the year 2000 we will undoubtedly be looking at an
even more complex world which will seem almost foreign to
the 1975 experience. There will be new industries, unheard of
processes, and unimaginable products. However, this new
world will be manned by the old people, and that in itself may
be the primary source of stress. The old people will not be
equipped to deal with the new world. And the new people will
not be equipped to deal with the old.

New Organizations

Bennis and others have suggested that the traditional
management model is not capable of dealing with change.
This bureaucratic form was fine at the onset of the industrial
revolution. But in terms of its capacity for dealing with
accelerated change, bureaucracy fails miserably. The democratic or participative form must replace the traditional
approach for dealing with high levels of complexity. And, in
this Toffler era of change, it would seem that the democratic
form should become more and more predominant.

But a couple of things are holding back the progress of
democracy in the work world. First, and perhaps most important, the bureaucratic structures of yesteryear were designed to
avoid change and thus to perpetuate themselves. This feature
added a great deal of stability which was surely needed at the
time. But it doesn't help to deal with progressive change. And,
second, most of us having been trained and educated within an
autocratic environment, find that it is very difficult, if not
impossible, to operate democratically within a participative
structure. So a very common picture which we see in the world

of work is one in which democratic process is held as an acceptable ideal, but never quite accepted as a behavioral mode. Perhaps it is the positive semantic value of the word democratic that clouds the whole issue, because most people, when asked about their own management styles, are quick to assert the participativeness of their approach. But, at the same time, it is also the universal experience of many of us, that when faced with a tough organizational issue, for example, the disciplining of a subordinate, we become very autocratic. This is a very normal process since we have all been exposed to countless examples of the apparent efficiency of an autocratic method.

Thus the newer and more democratic organizations, which we desperately need to address the highly complex issues of the seventies and eighties, are extremely slow in coming. Their progress is impeded by those of us who find a great deal of difficulty in dealing with democratic structure.

Organization: A Definition

Perhaps the most important problem at this particular point in the book is to evolve an acceptable definition of the term *organization* which is useful and viable in terms of the changes which have permeated the organizational sciences during the past decade. Clearly, this would have been a simpler task a half century ago since the question of what organization was, was inseparable from how it was organized. Each structure was a kind of stereotype bureaucracy of Max Weber. Organization, which was clearly related to business and industry, rather than a kind of universal human phenomenon, consisted of a number of tried and true rules which had been passed on through the experiences of the early industrialists. These business organizations formed the prototype for what we now regard as autocratic management.

Weber's bureaucracy was said to be analogous to a social machine. By utilizing the logical tenets of military organization one could insure efficiency, precision, speed, continuity, uniformity of operation, and equity in dealing with large numbers of people. The stability of the organization would offer potential and actual participants the possibility of a predictable career path. The characteristics of this bureaucratic approach as suggested by Weber were:

1. Fixed areas of jurisdiction within the organization.

2. Hierarchy or the existence of a system of super and subordinate, each having more authority and responsibility than the level below.

3. A systematic approach to filing or storing the official records of transactions.

4. An official system of jobs as offices which presuppose training both within and without the organization.

5. Administrative procedures that consist of a set of rules which are generally stable and hard to change.

6. Officials who hold offices spend a portion of their time defining and rationalizing their offices in terms of the overall system.

7. New members may view the bureaucracy as a predictable and stable career matrix.

Thus fifty years ago the term *organization* implied simply the bureaucratic concepts of Weber or by definition, "the function and the structural characteristics of theory X."

Since the Hawthorne Studies, however, the task of evolving a definition for the term *organization* has been vastly complicated by the separation of the concept "organization" from the concept "structure."

First, let us deal with the issue of *organization* itself. What is an organization? How does the definition of what an organization is interact with the people who exist within it? Perhaps the best way of viewing the organization is as a behavioral system, that is, a set of interrelated behaviors. As such there are three apparent levels of behavior which become components of the organization.

1. Individual behavior or the things that are done by the persons who belong to the organization

2. Group behavior or the manifestations of the groups which make up the organization

3. Organizational behavior: the characteristic actions of the organization itself as it deals with the components of its environment

Moving from this platform it might be suggested that:

Organization is the interconnection between individuals and groups who are pursuing one or more aggregate goals.

Beyond this definition, however, is the more important question of structure: "How is the organization interconnected?" Perhaps the best current strategy for describing the organizational approach is the autocratic versus the democratic criteria. A structure either is autocratic or democratic or somewhere in between. These two extremes are described below:

Autocratic		Democratic
1. Specialization	versus	Generalization
2. Standardization	versus	Nonroutine
3. Formal	versus	Informal
4. Central authority	versus	Shared authority
5. Hierarchy	versus	No hierarchy
6. Inflexibility	versus	Great flexibility
7. Downward communication	versus	Free directional communication
8. Decisions by leader	versus	Participative decisions
9. Motivation by rules	versus	Self-motivation
10. Emphasis on work	versus	Emphasis on people

The ten dimensions which are listed above describe the ways in which a democratic structure differs from an autocratic one. But let us expand upon this presentation by exploring each dimension individually.

Specialization is the key concept in the structuring of an autocracy. Almost by definition this kind of organization addresses itself to the assembly-line procedure of fragmenting itself into several different units each doing a particular aspect of the task. In a democratic organization, the opposite is true. The basic approach must be more generalized. Each phase of the organization must have a more broad understanding of what it can do. The second dimension, *standardization*, flows from the first. The process of specialization encourages the organization to continually refine its task in the hope that it can be made more consistent and predictable so that it can be more efficient. Democratic structures take the opposite approach. They must be able to work with the nonroutine problem.

The next four dimensions fit together in the sense of their impact on the organizations. Autocratic structures are, by necessity, more *formal* than participative. This stems from the fact that in the autocracy there is a *central authority* or one boss who is viewed by all as the leader. There is a great deal of *hierarchy*, the apparent existence of levels of authority between participant and leadership, and there follows a great deal of *inflexibility*. This inflexibility is in part related to the standardization and specialization, but it is also clearly linked to the hierarchy between bosses and workers. Democratic organizations take a very different structural approach. First of all, they tend toward informality. This is partially because of the lack of hierarchy. Since all participants operate at the same structural level (no hierarchy) the leadership role in a democratic structure is more like a coordinating function than it is like the traditional behavior which we tend to associate with leadership. Consequently, the authority which is inherent in a particular group or unit is shared and there is a great deal of flexibility in terms of what is to be done, who is to do it, and how it should be accomplished.

Autocratic organizations are further typified by downward patterns of communication. Most of the official messages which are sent within the organization pass from top to bottom with little feedback from the bottom. For all practical purposes the condition of *downward communication* seals off the upper levels of the hierarchy from the bottom. In this autocratic system *decisions are usually made at the top levels* of the hierarchy, *motivation to comply is by the rules,* and the overriding emphasis or "charter" for the unit is *to accomplish the task.* Democratic organizations, again, function in a very different way. In the democracy, communication is multidirectional. It works in every possible way since there is a corresponding de-emphasis of hierarchy. The emphasis in terms of participation is for each person to become involved in decisions about what is to be done, by whom, and when. Then the participants are counted upon to be self-motivated. While the work is being carried out there is a much greater emphasis upon the people who are doing the work than there would be in an autocratic organization.

So the second part of our understanding of what *organization* is involves the existence and description of structure:

> *Organizations* may be designed or structured in different ways. They may be highly autocratic, or highly democratic, or more commonly a combination of both autocratic and democratic structural components.

Man as an Unwilling Participant

We have seen something of the evolution of the organization as a dominant social form. This "thing" that we have struggled to define and to understand may, in fact, separate us from other forms of life on the planet, for man is the only organism that actually participates in the organizational process. Some other animals, notably chimpanzees, baboons, and dolphins, have evidently evolved to the level of sophisticated group activity. But only humans have linked groups together into large and complex good-seeking units.

It is also oversimplistic to think of organization as a phenomenon only linked to business or to manufacturing. The approach has indeed spread to every known aspect of human endeavor—to hospitals, schools, governments, churches, volunteer groups, recreational organizations, and sales and service agencies. Indeed, the world is a complex network of organizations. Some are large. Some are small. Many are democratic, while others are autocratic. But the fact remains that organizations comprise the context within which we all exist.

So each of us must begin at an early age to immerse himself or herself in the process of organizational life. Each of us must in some ways give up just a bit of his or her own identity to align himself or herself with an organization. This omnipresence of the organizational form is akin to the air which we breathe. We don't know how it affects us. We never gain an insight into how it influences our lives because we haven't experienced life without organizations. Perhaps this is why so little attention has been paid to the entire question of the "organization" and how it affects the individual. Or perhaps it is that we have so rapidly been overwhelmed by the growth or organizations. In any event, we have not reacted well. We have not learned to predict or to control the relationship between man and his organizational environment. Management is in its infancy.

And while both the theory and the practice of management struggle to understand this entire question, the unfortunate participants must suffer through some very stressful situations:

1. The question of whether an autocratic or a democratic structure should be employed

2. The pressure toward continually increasing technical and task complexity

3. The problem of human obsolescence

These are the issues which necessitate the integration of the study of stress with the study of management practice. It is the participant, each and every one of us, who ends up paying the price of progress. And we may be paying by the absorption of incredible volumes of stress.

To clarity this question, however, we must first review our understanding of management. What do we know about management? Where does this information come from? What is included in a modern theory of management? These are the questions which will be expanded within the next chapter.

chapter 2

Management as a Science

This field that we refer to as management has changed so radically in the past few years that it is easy to lose sight of the dynamic nature of our jobs as managers. What was good management practice only ten or fifteen years ago may be obsolete or worse today. And more importantly, those of us who work from day to day are faced with the almost impossible task of keeping up. This chapter will lay the groundwork for a discussion of job-related stress by defining the changing nature of management theory. Once this complicated view of management has been presented it will be simple within the following chapters to show how stress is related to our jobs. For now, however, let us proceed with the evolution of management and a discussion of contemporary management theory.

The Art of Management

In the early days of the industrial revolution the practice

of management was more of an art that a science. Managers were, in most cases, the owners of their enterprises. They typically came from an artisan background and maintained a degree of technical knowledge about their overall businesses that would be impossible in today's world. For example, the candle maker, who learned the art from his father, grandfather, and great-grandfather, came to a point where the age-old process was no longer competitive. He was forced to convert his art-form to a more mechanized assembly-line procedure. This industrial revolution lowered prices, increased supply, and, more importantly, converted an artist to a manager.

So the early managers were oriented toward art as an approach. Adding to this, their complete knowledge of their product, it was only natural that the early managers did not take a scientific approach to organizing, motivating, and controlling their enterprises. They did things their own way and many of them were very successful.

Transitions toward Predictability

As business and, perhaps more importantly, colleges and universities evolved, the interest in management increased. Many different academic disciplines began to focus their attention upon the process of management. And as management underwent the gradual transition from a human art to a bona fide academic pursuit, the pressure mounted for a predictable and scientific approach which could be presented to both students of the subject and practical working managers.

But the state of the art in the fifties and sixties[1] did not provide answers to many fundamental questions about the management of people. In fact the academies were in the middle of their own great debate about a basic approach to management. As we saw in the last chapter, the academicians as well as the working managers appeared to be divided into two different camps, classical versus human relations. And the field of management seemed to be doing more about explaining and qualifying the arguments than moving toward a solution.

Classical proponents argued that workers had to be motivated by external stimuli. Man is a rational economic being. He wants only to get money to satisfy his urges to consume. Thus he must be motivated to start and then to continue working through the use of either rewards or punishments or both. Left to his own devices man is likely to behave in a lazy way. Douglas McGregor[2] further typified man from the perspective of classical theory as selfish and self-fulfilling. He has his own goals and these goals are, by definition, contrary to the aims of the organization where he works. So classical proponents approach management in a unique way. Their strategy is to design an organization which controls the persons who work in it. The organization must provide incentives and punishments which manipulate the employees toward the grand goals of the overall organization.

Human-relations proponents take a very different view of the worker. They see him as a self-directed, and self-motivated person who can be expected to have goals which are in agreement with the goals of the organization itself. Thus the human-relations manager takes an approach which is different from that of the classical manager. He is a democrat! He spends his efforts working with his subordinates to coordinate their efforts rather than telling them what they must do.

And while the researchers were spending their efforts articulating the problem of classical versus human-relations management, the practicing managers were in a double bind. They were struck in the middle of real management situations and if they were to seek help in the management literature they could find any of several different answers to their problems depending upon whom they read. This was all the more reason for people to simply do what they felt was best. After all, the "experts" didn't have the answers either.

Contingency Theory

As the sixties began, however, several management theorists began to sense that the ultimate answer to how one should manage was not a single style at all, but a systematic approach.

The history of the classical versus human-relations argument
was filled with outstanding examples of success and failure on
either side. Thus it was reasoned that neither side was right or
wrong, but that each was situationally bounded.

Paul Lawrence and Jay Lorsch[3] from the Harvard
Business School designed and carried out a now famous set of
studies which were aimed at unraveling the conflicts between
the classical and human-relations camps rather than supporting one or the other.

They investigated several different kinds of management
approaches ranging from classical to human relations (and
including middle approaches) and found that the important
factor, in terms of determining success, was not the approach
itself but the appropriateness of the approach. The most
critical question surrounding the design of a management
strategy is "what are you going to do?" not "how are you to do
it?" Contingency theory suggests that:

> The style of management should be a function of the
> management task. Simple, predictable tasks with short-
> time perspectives ought to be approached with a classical
> management perspective. Conversely, complex, dynamic,
> and unpredictable tasks should employ a more demo-
> cratic or human-relations approach. Tasks which are
> judged to be somewhere between highly complex and
> simple require a middle approach.

A favorite classroom example of the management style
problem is the John Wayne-Wally Cox situation. John Wayne
is the perfect example of a classical manager. He conveys a
cinematic toughness and authority which most of us associate
with the typical autocratic leader. And in film after film he has
been supersuccessful in averting tragedy and accomplishing
success via this unique style. Time after time he seizes the
situation and determines a plan of action, tells people what to
do and how to do it, and wins in the end. Wally Cox, on the
other hand, is quite the opposite kind of character. He is a
meek, mild, democratic man by nature and his cinematic
successes are quite different at least in approach. He is a

coordinator. He is more concerned about people and their feelings than he is about success. And yet his batting record is more than respectable.

Here we have a good example of contingency theory at work—two different men, both successful but using different approaches for different kinds of situations.

Now it is possible to use stupid recruiting techniques to fill jobs with the wrong kinds of managers and, consequently, to guarantee failure. Let's assume, for example, that we want to find a director for a cancer research institute which employs several Ph.D.'s and M.D.'s in such fields as biochemistry and genetics.

If we were to select a John Wayne type character, what would happen? How would the employees react to the John Wayne approach? Contingency theory would predict failure. While John Wayne would do well in the typical "battlefield situation" he would not be effective in this particular position. Wally Cox, on the other hand, is cut out to administrate the complex-task kind of job. His democratic style which involves other people in goal setting and in job definition itself is exactly what is needed for the research director.

There are situations where Wally Cox would be doomed to failure and John Wayne could be a natural success. And finally, there are all kinds of situations which are mixtures of the John Wayne and the Wally Cox styles. They lie somewhere between the supercomplicated and the super simple. These are the kinds of management situations that most of us face on a day-to-day basis. And these are the situations that demand managerial proficiency.

A Practical Approach

The manager of the seventies needs to have a predicting tool at his disposal. He must have a model which sorts management theory into the most important components and then gives guidelines for practice. Such a tool follows. It is based upon the contingency-theory research of Lawrence and Lorsch and others, the leadership theories of Fred Fiedler,[4] and

my own research efforts. This simple set of steps has been
utilized by several hundred of my students and consulting
clients. And, while it is not a panacea, it represents a useful and
practical approach: one that can be learned and utilized by
anyone to great advantage.

Step 1. *Write down the goals of your unit.* This and the
following steps are equally applicable to a small department,
to a large organization, or to any kind of aggregation between
those sizes. But the smaller the unit the more practical and
operable these steps become.

Step 2. *Evaluate the task complexity of your unit.* To aid
this process use a five-point scale like the following one:

1	2	3	4	5
Very simple	Relatively simple	Average	Moderately complex	Very complex

First, the number and diversity of goals from Step 1 should be
an indicator of task complexity. A number-1 task is highly
stable versus changing, simple rather than complex, short
cycle instead of long cycle, easily learned and utilizing programs for problem solution rather than intuitive judgment.
The best example of this type of job might be a punch-press
operation where operators are making a single unit of production and turning out thousands of pieces an hour. The
number-5 job is the "cancer research" kind of task. The
problem is not well defined, approaches are not programmed,
job cycles are very long or perhaps never repeat themselves, and
many times intuition must be used to attack a particular
problem.

Step 3. *Choose the management style, the structure and
the personnel to match the task complexity.* If the task to be
done is a number-5 or complex task then the management style
should be human relations or democratic, the structure should
be participative or democratic, and the people who work in the
unit should be people who need a democratic environment to

be productive. Conversely if the job to be done is a number 1 in terms of task complexity, such as the punch press operation, then leadership should be classical (or autocratic), structure needs to be autocratic, and the personnel should consist of persons who have high needs for autocratic structure.

The Manager's Problem

This third step represents the manager's dilemma. Each of us, no matter what kind of organization we work in, is faced with three fundamental decisions:

1. What kind of leadership style?
2. What kind of structure?
3. What kind of personnel?

The contingency theory approach provides a useful technique for answering each issue. Given the kind of task, and it should be noted that in the real world of work most tasks are a mixture of simple and complex (thus measuring between 1 and 5), it is possible to predict the management strategy which will lead to success. Table 2.1 illustrates the kinds of managerial decisions which lead to organizational effectiveness or success given the kinds of task structures suggested previously.

Let me illustrate with an example of my own management dilemma as a college professor. Each of us who is in the business of educating students is faced with the same kinds of problems that face any other manager of people. There is a task to be done: teaching accounting or history or English literature. And there are three fundamental decisions to be made: The leadership or teaching style, the organization/class structure, and personnel selection. The observant reader may object that professors don't choose their students. That is correct but it is also true that managers don't usually select all of their employees.

Thus the first task of the teacher is to evaluate task complexity. If he or she teaches accounting, for example, the task may be a number 1 while a course in existential philosophy might rate a 4½. Different subjects convey different task complexities. Therefore, as in managing, there is no one

Table 2.1

The Manager's Problem

Evaluate Task Complexity	Manager's Fundamental Decisions		
	A. Select leadership style	B. Select the type or organization or group structure	C. Select the proper personnel
1 Simple, short-time perspective, stable, easily learned programs	Autocratic or military-style leader	Very autocratic or traditional, industrial engineering standards for everything	Needs autocratic environment and leadership for motivation
2 Fairly simple, moderate cycle time, difficult programs, training required	Fairly autocratic but gathers and digests information from participants	A great deal of standardization and hierarchy but more flexible than the above	Needs autocratic environment but with some flexibility for participation
3 Average complexity, analytical, programmable with effort	Mixed autocratic and democratic components	Mixed autocratic and democratic type, strong authoritarian leader and participating personnel	Needs mixture of autocratic and democratic structure to be effective

Table 2.1 continued

The Manager's Problem

Evaluate Task Complexity	Manager's Fundamental Decisions		
	A. Select leadership style	B. Select the type or organization or group structure	C. Select the proper personnel
4 Fairly complex, changing, long cycles, some guesswork required, somewhat unpredictable	Participative process but leader retains right of final decision	Relatively participative process but final authority rests with leader, very little hierarchy	Needs participative environment with some central authority
5 Complex, dynamic no cycles, intuitive and creative unpredictable	Democratic, leader acts as coordinator, has no more power than others	Absolute democracy, all participate in policy and decision process	Needs democratic environment to be productive

correct teaching style. Philosophy ought to be taught in a different way than accounting or geography or economics. It should be taught in the way that is appropriate in terms of the structure and the teaching style.[5] Accounting courses which are closer to 1 or 2 need to have relatively rigid and autocratic structures with a kind of military teaching style. Homework assignments, fixed schedules and outlines, and required reading lists are very appropriate. In other words subjects like first-year accounting or algebra are not taught by sitting around with coffee and having a "rap session." Some other kinds of subjects, however, can only be taught in this way.

So the teacher must determine a course structure and a teaching style that is appropriate for his or her own subject matter. The manager must also evolve a structure and style appropriate to his or her task.

The manipulation of a structure is a relatively easy task. Structure itself is inanimate. Its feelings can't be hurt. Neither is it a creature of habit. Thus, to a large extent, a manager, working with or through his staff, can make changes in the organizational structure. He or she can increase or decrease levels of hierarchy, encourage flexibility, or make changes in the authority patterns. But the other two aspects of management are quite different in terms of their relative adaptability to change.

The Management of Leadership Style

Perhaps the most sticky management issue revolves about the manager himself and his leadership style. Leadership, for as much as is written and said about it, remains an experientially learned phenomenon. Our patterns and styles of leadership begin to form at a very early age, perhaps as soon as we are aware of our surroundings. Our parents, our friends, teachers, movie heroes and TV stars, all influence our youthful concept of leadership. And, by the mature age of five or six, children not only understand what leadership and authority are all about, but they have formed judgments about good versus bad leadership.

Then comes the first job as a paperboy or grocery store bagger and by the time one has moved through these transitionary jobs to a professional position he or she has experienced several bosses. During these experiences he or she certainly makes many mental notes. "This person was a good boss because of these things that he did or that person was a bad boss because of these other things." So, by the time anyone enters his first position of leadership, he has formed some very strong opinions regarding leadership. In short, he has developed a leadership style.

Contingency theory suggests that leadership style can be measured on a continuum from "1," very autocratic, to "5," very democratic. In addition, it has been suggested that there are certain situations in which any of these styles can be effective. But, in the practical sense, we are talking about one leader and one job. What if he doesn't have the correct style?

The management of leadership style involves understanding and dealing with oneself. Thus, the first step toward improving this aspect of work performance is to learn what one's leadership style really is. A questionnaire which can be used to test your own leadership style is included in the appendix of this book. Your first step should be to fill out this instrument to learn about your own style.

Armed with an understanding of your leadership style you are ready to make some important judgments about your own job performance. What is your style? What kind of job do you do (1 or 2 or 3 etc.)? Do they match?

Chances are that when a person evaluates his own leadership style versus the requirements of his job, he will find a discrepancy of some sort. Perhaps he is a "2" and the job calls for a "3." Or perhaps he is a "4" and the job requirements are "2." There is no need to commit suicide or worse if you find yourself in one of these situations. Most persons find that they have a midrange leadership style. They do not score "1" or "5" on the leadership test, they score "3" or "3.2" or "2.7." This suggests that most of us can't be too radically different from our job needs. Perhaps the scalar difference will be a single point or less. Second, and more important, is the idea that "knowing what's wrong helps." Even if our style is not absolutely right for a certain situation, knowing the leadership style itself helps us predict our own weak areas—places where we would be likely to make mistakes.

Assume, for example, that a particular manager has a leadership style of "4" and that he is managing a "3" task. The problems here are likely to revolve about the manager's tendency to be more democratic than the situation warrants. He may tend to be uncomfortable because of the mixed nature of the task and, worse yet, he may approach the job in an overly democratic way.

So, first and foremost, the management of leadership style involves an introspective step. What is my own leadership style? How does that affect my job performance? Secondly, the technique can be used in the administrative sense, that is, to evaluate other leaders in an organization or to select a new supervisor for a particular position.

The Management of People

Just as each of us has a leadership style formed on the basis of his or her experiences, we also have a followership style. Effective people-management involves the selection and supervision of personnel whose job needs match the demands of their jobs. Some people have a preference for relatively autocratic work. Conversely, other people need a more democratic environment to properly motivate them. So the trick in supervisory management is to get the right people in the right places. Many leadership authorities agree that much of what has been referred to as bad work or immature behavior by employees is really bad management practice.[6]

A skillful manager must size up his personnel and assign them to the various parts of the unit's task which match their motivational needs. In the ideal case, a manager could recruit new employees to match the job demands. If it's a punch-press operation, for example, the supervisor would attempt to employ number 1 or 1½ people for the job since a more democratically oriented employee would surely be frustrated by the demands of the task itself and by the appropriate structure and leadership style.

But realistically speaking, supervisors hardly ever have an opportunity to start from scratch and recruit new employees.

They are usually plunged into an ongoing job environment with a staff which has already been selected. So, here are four practical rules of thumb to follow:

First: *Try to learn the followership needs of each employee.* There are several ways of doing this. If it is possible to have employees fill out a questionnaire without causing hard feelings, union grievances, or both, I suggest using the "Followership Style" instrument which is located in the appendix. If that is impossible, then the supervisor should at least try to form the best possible intuitive judgment of what each employee's followership style really is.

Second: *Use employees in different jobs according to their needs and skills.* No matter what the task structure is you will probably find that some aspects of the job are more or less predictable and complex than the average job within your unit. A maintenance supervisor, for example, has a program of preventive maintenance (a job which is predictable in nature) and at the same time a machine breakdown to attend to which may be much more complex and dynamic in terms of a task structure. Therefore he should assign different kinds of employees to these very different jobs. The preventive maintenance man can follow an autocratic program to accomplish his task, but the breakdown man had better be a self-starter.

Third: *Treat different people in different ways.* Now this one goes against the grain. We have always heard that to be "fair and square" we have to treat everyone equally. But actually that rule doesn't help anybody. Since the democratic fellow will need a participative leader and the number 1 employee requires the opposite treatment, it makes good supervisory sense to minister to their individual needs. You may be accused of being unfair by some of your employees, but if you make a practice of telling them why you are doing what you are doing they will probably begin to understand, at least in the long run. This strategy may also strain your psychological capacities since it could be at odds with your personal management style, so be careful to act within reasonable limits of your comfortability range. If you are, by nature, a 4 leader, don't try to pretend that you are a 1 because the result of that kind of dishonest leadership will be a very frustrated you.

Fourth: *Recruit properly.* When it does finally become your chance to add a staff member, remember the importance of the stylistic congruence which has been discussed. A new employee should fit into the entire job situation, meaning the task, the structure, and the leadership style which are ongoing in your department. This fit could be much more important than technical competence. I personally would rather hire an accountant to do an engineer's job than train an autocratic person to fit into a democratic situation.

The Dynamics of Management

A few final words need to be said about this contingency theory approach. First, it is very important to emphasize the neutral nature of all of these management components. There is nothing fundamentally good or bad about an autocratic boss, a democratic structure, a complicated task, or an employee who needs a number 2 job structure. "Good" is when the job gets done effectively and "bad" is when it doesn't. Thus good management is simply the matching of characteristics. Individual aspects of management such as an employee's leadership style should be measured but not evaluated!

Another important point is that all of these managerial components are very subject to change. This week a person is a "2," next month he may be a "3." Good management practice requires a constant reevaluation of task complexity, structure, leadership, and personnel.

And finally, good management many times means trying to strike a very delicate balance. Perhaps you are faced with a number 2 task but the existing staff is very democratic (5) in terms of their fellowship needs. The best managerial strategy might, then, be to evolve a structure which splits the difference between the needs of the job and the needs of the employees.

Scientific Management

Clearly, the theory of management has made some tremendous strides within a very short time. In just ten years we have moved from a kind of confused discipline which had little or nothing to offer in terms of good solid advice for the practical manager to a much more scientific and systematic field. Contemporary management theory has the capacity to explain many of the difficulties of past management practices as it offers a practical and sensible set of prescriptions for today's managers.

But the simple fact remains that most of the persons who work at management positions, have not had any formal training in leadership or management theory. They operate on the basis of their experiences, thus tending to manage in a way which would be very appropriate for themselves, that is, if they were somehow able to be supervisor and supervisee simultaneously. Unfortunately, however, the employees who happen to be exposed to this experientially based leadership style may have some very different kinds of needs. And consequently, many of these ad-hoc styles of management prove to be inappropriate.

Management practice, the total realities of life within most contemporary organizations, is lagging well behind management theory. And perhaps this is because managers have grown tired of reading through the turmoil which used to typify the leadership literature. Or perhaps it is simply because it is easier to manage in your own comfortable way, than it is to attend to the complex problem of gaining and executing leadership training. In any event, we might expect that organizations will continue to be filled with countless interpersonal problems which, to a large extent, are due to mismanagement. And not the least of these many human relations problems is stress!

We have spent these first chapters trying to unfold a picture of man at work. We have seen how the world of work has evolved, and then how management theory has developed within the past several years. The purpose of the next chapter will be to introduce and describe the notion of work-oriented stress. It is fairly obvious that our jobs provide a continuing source of anxiety for many of us, but how does this happen? What are the determinants or causes of stress at work?

chapter 3
Stress at Work

It is abundantly clear to those of us who watch the process of change at work that each of us pays the price for mismanagement. And that price is probably greater than most of us would even care to know. It would also seem that the industrial system which has so rapidly evolved during the last half century has, as the saying goes, some "good news" and some "bad news." The good news is that each of us enjoys an incredible amount of leisure time as well as a sizable basket of economic goods (relative to our neighbors in other parts of the world or to our ancestors). The bad news is that the new system which brings us these benefits is also exacting a large price in terms of both the physical and psychological well-being of man. Perhaps we are now entering a period where the emphasis will be placed less upon the technical aspects of an industrial revolution, and more upon the human aspects. We need to study man's relationship with this new environment—this organizationally oriented work culture. Maybe we should hire

Jacques Cousteau to study the workers at IBM or General Electric and then to tell us how we are polluting our people. I sometimes have the feeling that we know more about dolphins than we know about ourselves!

There are many possible approaches to the task of categorizing the impact of jobs upon people. This chapter will present one such approach. The following pages will be devoted to the discussion of eight distinct sources of stress at work:

1. The Psychological Contract
2. Careers and Their Toll
3. The Forgotten Family
4. Human Obsolescence
5. Organizational Obsolescence
6. Coping with the Job
7. Organizational Ideology

Each will be identified and discussed in terms of its impact upon people at work.

The Psychological Contract

The trouble with most jobs starts right at the critical transition period—the time immediately before taking the new job plus the first few weeks of work. For many of us a job change is motivated by an unsatisfactory situation at our existing job. Something is bothering us. Or something is not happening in the correct way. In short, the present job situation falls short of our expectations for one or more reasons.

The logical step then is to begin looking for a new job and it is then that our expectations for the new one begin to build. "The thing wrong with my present job is that I don't have enough responsibility!" So a primary expectation for the next job would include all of the positive aspects of the current job plus more responsibility.

The overall process by which people seek jobs, is incredibly complicated. Each of us faces the prospect of finding a job at least a few times during his life. And the mental set which we carry with us on this search is extremely complex. While this psychological job-expectation profile is certainly the unique result of our intellectual and experiential view of work, there is one simplifying aspect of the approach to work which can be regarded as both universal and useful. That is the *psychological contract.*[1]

Each person forms a unique series of expectations regarding his or her job. These come from a variety of sources including imagination, the objective image of the company, interviews with personnel officers and/or prospective supervisors, and other miscellaneous sources. While the psychological contracts of individuals are varied and complicated, one universal proposition can be forwarded:

> Each person forms a psychological contract with his place of employment and that contract, although not necessarily related to objective fact, acts as a motivating basis for the ongoing relationship between the employee and the job.

Now how can such a universal principle be useful for management? The answer is very simple. The psychological contract differs from an ordinary contract in that it exists only in the mind of the employee. Thus, the most useful (and at the same time rare) thing that a company or a manager can do is to encourage employees to articulate their own contracts. This has two immediate benefits. First, the manager has the opportunity to deal with problem areas within the mental framework of his employees. And secondly, the process of articulation allows each employee the opportunity to experience the complexity of his own demands and the difficult position of the company in trying to minister to these psychological needs.

All too often, however, the psychological contract is overlooked and employees become frustrated because of contract "violations" by employers who don't even realize the existence of the contract. I once spoke to a man who had stormed out of a very nice job because the company's personnel manager (who had since left his own job) had promised him a reserved parking place which he never received. While this is an extreme case, I suspect that a great many employee misunderstandings arise because of this psychological contract phenomenon.

In terms of the stress issue, this problem of hidden job needs represents the first root cause of work-oriented stress—a job which does not match expectations. And because of the complex and changing nature of both jobs and people this source of stress is a universal one. No job can hope to satisfy all of the needs or expectations of a healthy growing adult.

Careers and Their Toll

Perhaps more generic than the issue of the psychological contract is the basic question of *career*. What a man is and who a man is is so often linked to what he does, at least in his culture, that the career concept is imbedded in our very nature at an early age. Whether we become a corporate vice president or a plumber or a factory worker the images which surround our career choices are strong ones.

Nowhere is this more obvious than at a party where new people meet. When two men are introduced they almost always size each other up with such questions as: "Where do you work? What do you do there?" For women the problem of identification with a career is complicated by the more fundamental question of woman's role in life. Should she be a housewife or should she pursue a career in the working world?

Our culture has followed the lead of the industrial revolution. The life styles which we follow revolve about work systems such as the 8-to-5 workday or the five-day workweek. And our social pecking orders are closely related to occupational choice. (For example, the physician is a prestigious person while the street cleaner is not.) Think for a moment about the number of TV programs about doctors or lawyers versus the number of TV programs about factory workers or salesmen! Herein lies a key to the pecking order in our culture. We are almost led to believe that unless there is a popular TV series about a person who is doing our job, then we are a failure.

The emphasis upon career, success, and social prestige is inherent within our culture. Its influence begins as soon as we are old enough to watch TV. And as our occupational choices become more and more settled, the majority of us are exposed to two different kinds of stresses. First, why couldn't we have selected and joined a more prestigious or different occupation? How many times has someone said, "If only I could live my life over again I would really do a better job of it!" And a second more subtle stress also emerges. "What must I give up for the sake of success in my profession?"

William Whyte's book, *The Organization Man,*[2] probably took the first systematic look at this question of career price. Many other writers have also noted the same general problem, that success within a profession usually involves giving up some things that are important to a person. The price then that we pay for our career is expressed in terms of the aggregate frustrations felt for things that have been "given up" for the sake of a career which is many times a second choice.

The executive, for example, is often caught up in a casual overtime problem. He feels that he is giving up his leisure for a career and that persons who do not conform to his 60-hour workweek are not pulling their share of the load. Thus he is subjected to all kinds of different stresses. "Why am I working on Sunday rather than playing golf? Fred and Pete went to play golf—the loafers, they should be in here working like me!"

The Forgotten Family

Perhaps the most universal cost of a successful professional career lies in the quality of family life. The executives that I have known almost universally complain about their unsatisfactory home lives. The job exerts pressure on the man to spend more time at work, while the wife and children exert pressure for more time to be spent at home.

The unfortunate executive is trapped right in the middle. If he leans toward the career his family suffers, if he prefers to concentrate more attention toward his family then he runs the risk of professional disaster. If he tries to walk a center line he will most probably feel that he isn't doing a good job at either.

I recently interviewed a top-level banking executive who unfolded the following incredible but perhaps typical story. He was about to leave for an expense-account two-day trip to a well-known Carolina golf-hotel resort to entertain some business clients. But he frankly stated that he would prefer to have hot dogs and beans with his wife and children for two days while he dug ditches. The ultimate paradox, however, was that when he returned to work his junior colleagues would be grumbling about the "all-expenses-paid" golf vacation that some lucky guys get. I wanted to ask him why he didn't quit that job and get one which would be less demanding, but I didn't!

There would seem, at first glance, to be only two basic choices available to the typical working person. First, to actively pursue a socially acceptable and financially rewarding career. The price of this selection would seem to revolve about alienation from the family. Or, second, to work a low-key modest kind of job and face the kinds of stresses which are associated with a low level of financial and socioeconomic status.

Human Obsolescence

The fourth component of stress relates to the process of change. Modern man must learn to cope with an increasing process of change. Warren Bennis[3] has suggested that this change which includes social, technical, and educational progress is proceeding at a geometric rate. In other words, modern man may view more change in a year than his grandfather saw in a lifetime. Alvin Toffler[4] uses the example of the speed of travel. In 6000 B.C. the top speed available was the camel caravan which traveled at eight miles per hour. This was not improved upon until the invention of the chariot in 1600 B.C. The steam locomotive (1825) traveled at thirteen mph. But by 1880, sophisticated steam locomotives were moving at one hundred mph. Sixty years later, men were flying at four hundred mph. By 1960, in only twenty years of elapsed time, this speed changed to 18,000 mph for men in space capsules.

The message here from Toffler and Bennis is that mankind is both facing and trying to cope with an incredible barrage of change. And perhaps this change has its greatest impact at work. Working people are thrust into this avalanche of change and asked to do a good job, which usually implies keeping up with changes in their field. But many times the pressures of the job itself prevent one from taking the required time to monitor and adjust to changes within a profession. So it is not unusual to find an engineer, for example, who takes an honest look at himself after five or ten years in the field and concludes that he is hopelessly obsolete—that the younger engineers who are just graduating from college have a better grasp of the profession than he does.

Perhaps this explains the engineer-to-manager career path which seems to be so popular. And if, in fact, engineers and other technical people are making the transition to management or supervisory positions to flee from change, they soon find that they are not escaping a technology but moving to a new one. And this new "human" technology is probably even more foreign and confusing to them than the one which they have just left.

Thus, it is not hard for the average person working at either a professional or nonprofessional job to begin to feel obsolete after only a few short years of working. In the case of the lower level or nonprofessional employee the feeling is motivated by seeing the result of rapid change and not understanding it. For the professional or technical person the stress is more often the result of a growing feeling of datedness in terms of the profession itself.

As an executive once put it, "Who has time to read technical journals and stay up-to-date when he has a job to do?" And so the process of working eventually renders us incapable of continuing our work. Meanwhile, the stresses mount. It is not easy to be placed in these "damned if you do, damned if you don't" situations.

Organizational Obsolescence

Another major source of stress for most of us comes from the dynamic nature of the relationship between task structure and organizational structure which was discussed in the previous chapter. Ours is a long-standing tradition of autocratic (classical) organizational structure. This strong tradition has evolved from the turn-of-the-century industrialization which saw relatively simple patterns of work that were very successfully accomplished via autocratic management structures. Thus, we have learned from our experiences that the autocratic-formed organization is a highly efficient and successful approach to the problem of management, and we have oriented our entire supporting culture to this limited approach. Most of us have been educated in an autocratic setting, raised in an autocratic family, watched and participated in autocratically oriented activities (football, Little League, Boy Scouts, etc.) and have gone to work for autocratic companies.

But as Bennis and others have suggested, patterns of work have changed very rapidly—more rapidly, in fact, than our organizations can adjust. So organizational structure is out of tune with its task. Tasks are rapidly moving down the contingency-theory continuum from simple (1) to complex (5). Meanwhile, structures are remaining relatively constant. Organizational designers have learned from their past experiences that the autocratic structure works, so they are not about to change. Added to this is the dual problem of built-in resistance to change both by the design of the structure and the training of the participants. And the overall result is more stress!

We are like the carpenter who insists on driving nails with a screwdriver. As long as managers and workers alike use the wrong tool (the autocratic organization) for the job of doing complex work, we will continue to face a great deal of stress.

Coping with the Job

As we saw in the last chapter, modern management theory has just started to make significant progress in dealing with issues such as personnel placement. Each person who enters the world of work has a complex profile of very real needs surrounding his or her approach to a job. Although the autocratic-democratic continuum may be an oversimplification of this process, it is still a useful analytical framework. Some people have a need for relatively predictable work patterns, for short-cycle times, and programs for carrying out their jobs. Others are the opposite in terms of their needs for a job. And if a person finds himself working in the wrong kind of job relative to his needs, he will be frustrated by this experience.

Unfortunately, management practice has not caught up with management theory in this regard. Our work culture is filled with all kinds of complicated stimuli related to the problem of job selection. Money, status, security, career, and promotion opportunity all provide random and complex inducements for individuals to take certain jobs. But neither these criteria nor the typical organization itself is tuned into the most important question: What are the psychological needs of the worker? So, consequently, most of us spend a lifetime bouncing from job to job and experiencing a great deal of job-related stress. We change jobs for unclear reasons, and find ourselves in an endless series of different situations, none of which is probably better than the previous one. And the problems almost always lie within the reasons why we chose the job. We don't typically understand our own psychological needs. How many times have you heard of a person who is looking for a slightly more programmed job routine, or a situation which is just a bit more predictable? And personnel offices are usually so hopelessly bogged down with paperwork that they don't have time to explore the personnel-placement problem in terms of the needs of the employee either. So the worker is left floundering amid a random system of jobs and careers.

This job-needs-versus-stress framework may partially explain two very common experiences in the working world. First, there is the worker either at the management or nonmanagement level who gets into a very comfortable job and never changes. We have all seen examples of this phenomenon and probably questioned the whole process. "What's the matter, doesn't he have any ambition? Doesn't he want to get ahead?" Perhaps these are the few lucky individuals who blunder into jobs which are just perfect for them. They may recognize this compatibility and choose to trade "success" for comfort.

A second phenomenon is "resistance to change." How often have we all run into a person or group of persons who resist change at all costs? Perhaps change-avoiders do so in order to keep their relative level of job compatibility from deteriorating. People intuitively recognize a certain level of compatibility, so they resist the change.

Coping with the Boss

In light of modern leadership theory it is becoming very clear that a person's relationship with his supervisor may be the most critical aspect of job satisfaction and productivity. And again, management theory has begun to provide some very specific guidelines for supervisory management. But as in the issue of job selection, little or no attention is paid by most organizations to the problem of matching employees, at either upper or lower levels, with supervisors. Each of us has very specific needs for the kind of boss who will provide him with a good motivational climate. Organizations of all kinds could vastly improve their performance if they were to attend to this problem.

Instead, however, the issue of the supervisor-supervisee relationship is usually left to random chance. And the result is often disastrous. At the level of job performance itself, the result can be measured simply in terms of poor output. But, for the employee, the results of bad supervisory management are measured in terms of stress.

Organizational Ideology

A final and perhaps major issue which affects the level of work-related stress is the organizational ideology or conscience of the individual. When a person goes to work for an organization he goes through a gradual switching process where he transfers his personal ideology to an organizational ideology. He begins to identify with the place where he works in terms of both what it is and what it should be doing. And just as we might imagine a theological or moral framework within the personal life of a person, we can also conceive of this organizational ideology which serves as his personal framework for evaluating organizational behavior. In short, each person develops some strong feelings about what his company should or should not be doing. These feelings operate at many levels. First there is the immediate department or unit. "What are my department's objectives? Do I agree with them?" Second, there is the overall concept of the organization itself. "What is my company doing in this community or in the world?" These are issues which most employees of organizations are almost constantly grappling with.

In my own research I have found that the organizational ideology framework is a very powerful one for predicting leadership effectiveness perceptions and for predicting job satisfaction.[5] Employees at all levels of organizations tend to judge their companies, their immediate supervisors, and other top managers on the basis of their own ideologies for the organization. If they view managers as pursuing objectives which fall in line with their own ideological framework for the company then they judge them to be very effective managers. But if they perceive them to be pursuing organizational goals which are contrary to their own, they tend to regard them as ineffective leaders.

While employees of organizations continue to incorporate the objectives of their places of work into their own ideological frameworks, the organizations are becoming more and more fragmented. For almost all of us, the organizations where we work are increasingly growing larger and more out of control. We don't work in small, easily understood, single-product groups anymore, but in superconglomerates. And the price here, as in the previous factors within this chapter, is stress. As the organization becomes larger and less within the control of any of us, the pressure mounts against our organizational ideologies. In other words, it becomes almost impossible for us to be able to agree with the goals and aspirations of our organizations. The result is still another major source of stress— devoting our time and energy to a cause which we don't necessarily believe in.

The Organization and Stress

We have seen some very powerful reasons for the dramatic increase in the level of stress which is inherent in our job environments. Most of these are connected, at least in a general way, to the fact that the places where we work have grown so fast that we have not been able to continue to adapt ourselves to them. Each of the eight sources of stress, which we have just viewed, is a relatively new problem. In fact the turn-of-the-century workers probably would not have faced these particular dilemmas at all. The job of organizational designers in future years will be to develop approaches to management which will effectively solve these kinds of difficulties so that employees will be protected from the stresses and strains which are now apparent in most large organizations. But, in the meantime, each of us who work is going to be facing quite a large volume of stress at work.

Kahn, Wolfe, Quinn, Snoek and Rosenthal[6] capture the seriousness of the problem in the beginning pages of their book *Organizational Stress,* when they report that in a nationwide study of stress and anxiety at work, only one in six persons claimed to be relatively free of stress. The remaining 83 percent reported that they felt they were experiencing a great deal of stress as a result of their jobs. The stress studies which were done by Kahn et al. provide an important complement to the work that has been presented here, since these studies deal more particularly with the impact of stress upon the individual employee. The work which has been presented so far in this chapter represents a macrostress analysis, while the work of the Kahn group provides more of a microview of stress at work. Together the micro and macro studies represent a systematic view of job-related stress.

Role Conflict and Ambiguity

The Kahn studies, taken together with the prior discussion of organizationally induced stress, provide an over-all model for work-related anxiety which is shown in Figure 3.1. At the most general level are the secondary stresses. These come from the overall pressures which relate to career or family as well as more direct organizational difficulties, such as the issue of organizational ideology. The specific stresses of inappropriate jobs and supervisors provide the primary, less general, sources of stress at work. These eight stressors (which are the eight that were represented at the beginning of the chapter) comprise the aggregate sources of stress from the job environment.

Stressors have an impact on the person, but they are mediated by various factors within his personality such as the level of neurotic anxiety, rigidity, introversion or the motivational framework. They then work through the personality to cause both role conflict (or ambiguity) and stress.

This view of stress as related to role ambiguity quite naturally begins with the role-model approach to viewing interpersonal processes within an organization. Each person is seen as the focal point of many role relationships. His own role (the behavior expected from a person in a particular position) is complicated by at least two different factors. First, there is the way in which he sees himself in terms of position and the kinds of things required of him within that position. Second, there is the role which he perceives that another individual expects of him. And as if these two, often different, sets of role responsibilities are not confusing enough, there is also a very complex communications process. The role sender may

Figure 3.1
Determinants of Stress

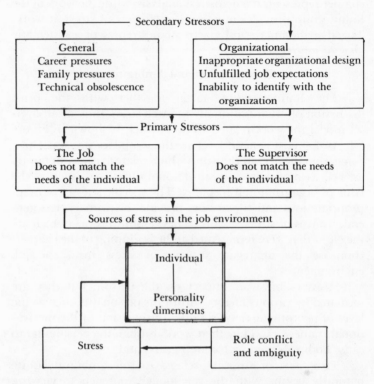

attempt to portray an image which is somehow different from his own. And finally the role receiver may complicate the issue by portraying an expectation which is not entirely his own.

We can begin to see, then, the complexity of role relationships in an organizational setting. For every interacting set of persons, there are four roles of work at any one time.

A. From the role sender

1. Ideal role—what he is (and should be) doing at the job

2. Sent role—what he wants another to think that he is (and should be) doing at the job

B. From the role receiver

1. Ideal role—what he thinks the role sender is (and should be) doing at the job.

2. Sent role—what he wants the role sender to think that he wants him to be doing at the job.

Moving from this role-set model, an organization can be viewed as a supercomplex network of role relationships. Naturally the role relationships do not transcend the issue of hierarchy. Role relationships are clearly affected by boss to subordinate or the subordinate to subordinate nature of the interpersonal process.

Many theorists have observed that the problem of role expectations, and more particularly role ambiguity, provides a major source of stress. Persons who become involved in complex organizations soon find that their jobs make many different kinds of role demands simultaneously. These complex role requirements cause a great deal of ambiguity in terms of a person's approach to his job. And the ultimate effect is stress.

The relationships between role conflict and stress are pictured in the lower part of Figure 3.1. The primary and secondary job stresses, mediated by personality, result in increasing levels of role ambiguity which, in turn, causes higher levels of stress. The relationship is also shown as self-sustaining, meaning that higher levels of stress reduce the capacity of the personality to deal with role ambiguity. Thus we may have a kind of vicious-cycle effect with stress causing more and more stress.

The Personality and Stress

Kahn et al. also investigated the impact of personality upon role ambiguity and stress. They particularly looked at the effect of four factors: neurotic anxiety, extroversion-introversion, flexibility-rigidity, and motivational orientation. They, as well as a number of prior researchers, had observed that certain individuals seemed to have a better (at least in terms of the external manifestations of stress) capacity to deal with complex situations than others. So they reasoned that

personality must have a significant effect upon organizational
stress. The following pages will include analysis of each of
these four personality factors.

Neurotic Anxiety

Many psychologists and psychiatrists have been concerned
with this particular dimension of personality. Viewed as the
opposite of emotional stability, neurotic anxiety is usually
thought of as a combination of excessive and conflicting
motivations, low self-concept, emotional instability, and the
inability to cope.

The Kahn research found that persons who were high in
neurotic anxiety also had a sensitivity to organizational stress.
In other words, they had a lower tolerance than their more
stable counterparts to stressful situations. Because of their
greater dependency needs, however, high-anxiety persons are
not apt to let stress lead to an erosion of their interpersonal
relationships. The other half of the finding was even more
interesting to the overall study of stress. Katz and his colleagues
determined that persons who were low in neurotic anxiety
were found to exhibit the symptoms of high-neurotic anxiety
when exposed to stress at their jobs.

In short, then, stressors from the organizational
environment would seem to cause an increase in neurotic
anxiety which in turn results in a reduced tolerance for stress.

Extroversion-Introversion

Another personality dimension which has attracted quite
a lot of attention is the extroversion-introversion characteristic.
It has long been held, at least in the mythology of organizations, that the dynamic, outgoing type of person has a better
capacity for dealing with organizational stresses, and that it is
the poor, quiet engineer off in the corner somewhere, who both
contributes in a major way to the important work that must be
done and is, at the same time, overwhelmed by the political
realities of organizational life. The Kahn research supports
this general understanding of extroverts versus introverts at

work. The extrovert appears to be better equipped to deal with stress than his introverted counterpart. He tends to see problems and anxieties as part of the organizational environment rather than of himself.

Kahn and his colleagues also uncovered some very interesting new understandings of the introverted person. It is not true that this less socially agressive type person does not desire to have or to maintain a set of high-quality interpersonal relationships. In fact there is every reason to suggest that the differences between introverted and extroverted persons have much more to do with problem-solving styles than with social needs. The withdrawal behavior of the more introverted person may very well be a defense mechanism for dealing with stress. Thus, the essential difference between the introverted and extroverted persons at work might be measured primarily in terms of their varying reactions to stress. The extrovert would appear to be relatively unaffected by stress, while the introvert tends to withdraw from relationships and then be perceived by his colleagues as antisocial and/or arrogant.

Flexibility-Rigidity

This dimension is so closely related to the autocratic-democratic dimension that, in my own judgment, the conclusions of the research done in this area are directly applicable to the management continuums previously presented. The stressors and the stress reactions of the rigid person are quite similar to those of the autocratic or #1 person, and vice versa.

The flexible person is defined as one who is outer-directed and participative rather than self-oriented, close-minded, and indecisive. The rigid person, on the other hand, is more concerned with authority systems than with the people who surround him. He is decisive, dogmatic, disciplined, and persistent.

Naturally each of these two very different types of persons is affected in a unique way by different kinds of stresses. The autocratic individual is most bothered by work-load problems or inequities, while the more democratic person tends to be stressed by role-overload difficulties. The Kahn research showed that democratic individuals are most affected by stress. The nature of their approach to work encourages ever-increasing role conflicts, particularly in times of peak workloads. Also, the more flexible person is more likely to respond to role-overload situations by experiencing greatly increased levels of anxiety. The more autocratic person, on the other hand, reacts to role conflict by rejecting those who are causing the conflict. Since his style is more work-directed or task-oriented, this rejection of collegues apparently doesn't cause his level of stress to increase.

We might conclude, then, on the basis of the Kahn findings, that democratic persons are more prone to organizational stresses than their autocratic counterparts. Consequently, the higher the level of democracy and/or flexibility the greater the danger of stress from a complex organizational environment.

Motivational Orientation

Kahn and his colleagues concluded their research by investigating the relationship of a number of basic motivational characteristics to stress.

Two broadly different sets of reactions were observed in terms of the motivational characteristics. Status-oriented individuals and expertise-achievement-oriented persons (both of which are said by Kahn to be much like the classic achievement-oriented individual) are severely affected by role conflict. Organizational stresses resulted in high levels of stress or tension for these persons. Security-oriented individuals, however, reacted quite differently. They did not appear to be significantly influenced by stress from their organizational environments.

Stresses and Personality: A Summary

It might be concluded, therefore, that the composition of a person's personality has a significant impact upon the relationship between organizational stressors, and the level of stress which is manifested by specific individuals. It would appear that some persons are much more affected by stresses within their environments than others. The stress-prone and stress-resistant personalities are pictured in Figure 3.2.

The evidence presented by Kahn and his colleagues does not support a proposition that certain individuals are stress-

Figure 3.2
The Personality and Stress

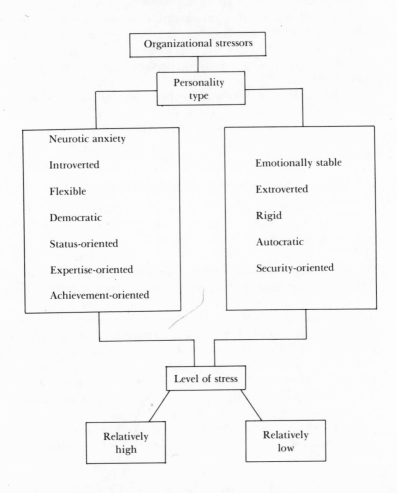

proof. In fact, the indications are quite the opposite. Each of the dimensions discussed previously would appear to be a two-ended continuum. One end of the continuum is usually stress-prone while the opposte end tends to be more stress-proof. There are two characteristics of these stress-related personality dimensions which lead to difficulty for most of us. First, most of us do not lie at extreme ends of the continuums. Instead, our actual personality measures are usually closer to the centers, thus making almost all of us at least somewhat stress-prone. And second, the various personality dimensions which are associated with the low-stress personality type are not necessarily correlated. And that suggests that most of our personalities are composites of relatively stress-free and stress-prone dimensions.

The implication for the individual is simply that each one of us is subject to various levels of stress on the basis of our complex individual personality type. We cannot hope to be stress-free. Thus we must learn to recognize and deal with stress.

Everyman: A Man in the Middle

All of the evidence so far leads to one basic conclusion: each and everyone of us is constantly subjected to an incredible barrage of stress. The stressors come from many different parts of an increasingly complicated environment. And while there is some hope that management theory can develop to the point where it can at least mediate the serious damage done by the misadministration of our present organizations, the prospects of this being an immediate reality are bleak at best.

So the ulcers and heart attacks and hypertension continue to plague our colleagues at work. They are the price which we pay for success. The message which we usually fail to hear, however, is that we are next. Yes, that's right. The ulcers and heart attacks will someday affect us just as surely as they have affected our bosses. The only question is when!

The next section of the book is designed to answer these questions. And the answers are both hopeful and exciting!

part 2
The Impact
of Stress

chapter 4

The Psychophysiology of Stress

So far we have focused our attention primarily upon the development of management theory. Our discussion of stress to this point has been very incomplete in that it has neither treated stress as it affects the individual nor made a systematic definition of the concept.

The purpose of this chapter is to introduce the notion of stress from the perspective of the person who experiences it. What is stress, how does it affect me, and how does my level of stress affect my work? These are the kinds of questions that will be answered here.

Part of the impetus for this study of stress at work and its impact upon the "whole person" quite naturally came from my own experiences at work. During my ten assorted years of engineering and teaching within a number of different organizations, I have gotten to know several relatively young men who suffered unexpected heart attacks. Two common trends struck me about these people who were working at different kinds of jobs in different places and times. Each victim was a superconscientious, hard-working, and apparently over-worked fellow. And the timing for his heart attack coincided perfectly with seasonal peak workloads. For the teachers, it was final-exam time. For the public accountant, it was inventory time. It seemed paradoxical that each was stricken at the exact time when he was most needed in his job.

But was this really a coincidence? Or could there not be a strong relationship between the job and the physical and psychological health of its incumbent? And worse yet, was this the reward for doing a good conscientious job?

My research since then has suggested that there are, in fact, some very clear relationships between the overall "health" of a person and his job. These can be measured and predicted in terms of stress. But, perhaps it is more important to emphasize the fact that a person can gain control of this situation and overcome the impact of work stress. He can be a competent and active person in the working world without giving up his emotional and physical well-being. And it is to this end that the rest of this book is devoted.

An Introduction to Stress

In the last chapter we isolated several causes of stress at work, and we linked them with existing management theory. But, realistically speaking, when we get involved in the day-to-day mechanics of working at a job, all the theory in the world is not useful. What is needed, instead, is a simple understand-ing of what stress is all about in terms of what it does to us.

Actually stress is a fairly familiar concept in the context of mechanics. Every beginning physics student has addressed the notion of stress within a physical system. In this context, the term *stress* is described as a measure of strain or force which tends to change the shape of the body upon which it acts until that body fractures or breaks. The popular children's party game of "sitting on the balloon until it breaks" is a classic example of applied stress. If the child sits on the balloon in just the right way he increases the total stress on the system to the point where the balloon must finally rupture.

In 1936 the British journal *Nature* published the first reference to stress in the human system under the title, "A Syndrome Produced by Diverse Nocuous Agents." Generally speaking, this stress concept which was pioneered by Dr. Hans Selye,[1] was similar to our balloon example. People were said to be subject to stress which could deform the human system and also, in some exaggerated cases, could cause that system to break.

As a young medical student, Selye observed that the process of identifying any particular kind of disease on the basis of symptoms was an extremely difficult one. Each patient who was presented for diagnostic treatment had symptoms that were common with every other patient. Fever, nausea, aches and pains, loss of appetite, skin rashes and swollen spleens or livers were almost universal symptoms of each patient. The great trick within the general problem of diagnosis was to isolate one or two unique symptoms so that they could be linked to a particular disease.

So while the practice of medicine continued to focus upon the search for a unique symptom, Selye became enraptured with the sickness syndrome itself. A sick person simply looked, acted, and felt sick. Was it possible that this sickness (later to be called stress) syndrome could exist independently of any particular disease? And, if so, what was the cause?

In his early work Selye encountered so much resistance to the term *stress* (as used within the notion of a stress syndrome) that he employed different terminology. At first he used the name *GAS*, or *general adaptation syndrome*, to cover a three-stage process consisting of:

1. The alarm reaction
2. The stage of resistance
3. The stage of exhaustion

The process, as described by Selye, begins with a confrontation by some kind of a stress agent. If the body can withstand this original attack without suffering instant death, it then

calls to attention all of its biological protective systems in order
to fight off this stressor. And, when the attack is overcome, the
body moves to a second state where it works at rebuilding its
reserves while it continues to fight off the continuing stress
attack. But finally the organism wears itself down to the point
where it can no longer fight off the continuing attack and
simultaneously attempt to build itself back up. This is the
beginning of a third and final stage of exhaustion. At this
point a kind of premature aging takes place followed by the
ultimate death of the organism. Since the body can no longer
build its reserves, the stresses begin to eat away at the body
itself.

This is the process by which Selye views stress. Persons are
constantly under attack from all kinds of nonspecific as well as
specific agents in their environments. The telephone at work,
the hostility of a coworker, changes in temperature, viral
infections are just a few of the many factors which can affect
us. As we are attacked by these various agents our bodies
automatically proceed through the three stages of the stress
syndrome. And perhaps the reason that we finally get a cold,
for example, is that our body just can't handle an additional
attack without slipping so deeply into the alarm-reaction stage
that the symptoms of the stress syndrome begin to manifest
themselves.

Dr. Herbert Benson of the Harvard Medical School has
pioneered the study of stress as related to business men in
particular. His work suggests the same kind of phenomenon
that was cited by Selye. Benson proposes that man's close
relationship to the animal world implies the existence of many
physiological mechanisms that are common requirements
throughout the animal world. One of these instincts which
man shares with his relatives is the fight-or-flight response.

> When an animal perceives a threatening situation, its reflexive
> response is an integrated physiological response that prepares it for
> running or fighting. This response if characterized by coordinated
> increase in metabolism (oxygen consumption), blood pressure, heart
> rate, rate of breathing, amount of blood pumped by the heart, and
> amount of blood pumped to the skeletal muscles.[2]

According to Benson, stress reactions are continually built up within all of us because our fight-or-flight responses are overstimulated. Thus our bodies get themselves into a kind of perpetual stress situation where they are constantly being confronted by stimuli which cause fight-or-flight reactions.

As a mechanism for survival, this response was, and continues to be, quite useful at least for most of the members of the animal world. Perhaps a good example of this process can be found within the behavior of the white-tailed deer, an animal which is very common in the forests of Pennsylvania, my own home state. Whenever I walk through the interior of Presque Isle State Park, which is located almost within sight of my office window, I will invariably encounter at least a few of these magnificent animals. Their reaction to me is very predictable. When they sense that I am near they change to a very erect position for just a split second and then burst into a full gallop through the woods. That split second allows the animal to instinctively decide upon one of the two courses of action, fight or flight. And the usual strategy, at least for this creature, is flight.

However, there have been a few occasions when the deer took a different tack. Last year, one of these animals, probably from the nearby state park, wandered onto our campus and jumped into the sunken gardens of our library building from which he could not escape. After a few confusing moments, the deer attacked the building ferociously blasting large holes in the thick glass windows which overlook the garden terrace. As he entered the library through one of the broken windows, students and librarians quickly retreated to safety. Needless to say, he was in an extremely violent mood. Before he left (through another large window) he succeeded in causing thousands of dollars in damage to the interior of the building. In another and more tragic case, a man who inadvertently hit a deer with his car was killed by the injured animal when he got out of his car to help it.

The point is clear. Animals, including the human being, possess and use a very useful mechanism called the fight-or-flight reaction. This instinctive part of us helps to negotiate dangerous situations by either giving us the physical power to flee, or making us a ferocious fighter. Even the most meek and gentle creature can become a "tiger" when cornered. For the animal in the forest, this useful reaction allows it to continue to exist by helping it make accurate and spontaneous decisions about dangerous situations. But for the person who operates within an organized society, this instinct can be counterproductive to say the least.

The deer which blundered into our library building is an excellent example of the counterproductive potential of a fight-or-flight response. I am sure that no one wanted to see that particular animal harmed. Most everyone who was near the deer when it wandered downtown simply wanted to help it return to its home in the forest. But the deer's instincts did not allow it to understand the situation. It felt that it was in danger. And consequently, it suffered a great deal of pain and anguish.

Man's position is potentially more dangerous, since it is one step further removed from the instincts of the deer. He has ceased to be aware of the existence, or the impact, of his fight-or-flight response system. Thus in his situation of deadened awareness, he runs the great risk of operating with a perpetually engaged fight-or-flight mechanism.

Toward a Definition of Stress

For a scientific definition of the term *stress* we again turn to Dr. Selye who invented the term, and whose work has helped the entire scientific community to understand and deal with the stress syndrome. Selye suggests that:

> Stress is the state manifested by a specific syndrome which consists of all the nonspecifically induced changes within a biological system.[3]

Now let us approach the components of this very clear and, at the same time, very difficult definition. First, stress is a state. It is not a heavy weight, or a particular reaction, or an anxiety, but a condition of being. Second, it is manifested by a specific syndrome or set of mechanisms within the body. This suggests that stress results in a certain pattern of physiological and psychological changes such as gastrointestinal, glandular, and cardiovascular disorders. And finally, stress, according to Selye, is nonspecifically induced. This means that it is caused by many different and changing agents. Moreover it affects the entire body, not just a single part. If I were to lift a heavy weight with my right arm, the resultant muscular change could not be categorized as stress since that weight represents a specific load upon a single muscle group. This entire process is pictured in Figure 4.1.

Selye is also quite emphatic about the fact that stress is not nervous tension. Although nervousness might be one of several parts of the stress syndrome, it is not, as many have suggested, synonymous with stress.

The Price of Stress

Those of us who live in this action-packed and highly paced Western culture pay a price. We pay in daily installments. Our jobs, our economic stability, even our leisure activity provide a constant barrage of stressors which affect our entire being. Since this stress which we absorb is subtle as well as constant, we don't suddenly find that we are stressed individuals. Instead the stresses sneak into our lives, and for many of us the final realization either never comes to us or it comes to us at a very late age. So we continue to pay our installments of stress. And this price is not simply paid in terms of our physical well-being. Stress affects our psychology, our emotional health, and our physical health simultaneously. Selye has performed laboratory experiments which suggest that the stress syndrome is a factor in the following diseases:[4]

1. High blood pressure
2. Heart disease
3. Blood vessel disorders
4. Diseases of the kidney
5. Eclampsia
6. Rheumatic and rheumatoid arthritis

Figure 4.1
The Stress Reaction

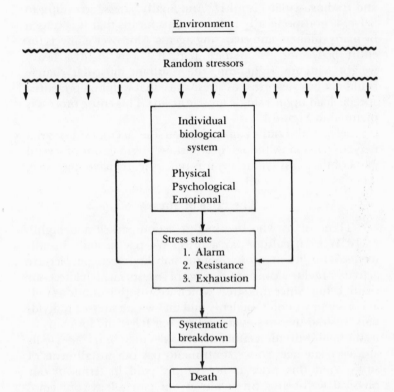

Environment

Random stressors

Individual
biological
system

Physical
Psychological
Emotional

Stress state
1. Alarm
2. Resistance
3. Exhaustion

Systematic
breakdown

Death

7. Inflammatory diseases of skin and eyes
8. Infections
9. Allergy
10. Nervous and mental disease
11. Sexual derangements
12. Digestive disease
13. Metabolic disease
14. Cancer
15. Diseases of resistance

It is not suggested that these diseases are solely or even fundamentally caused by stress reactions within the body. Selye has simply provided experimental evidence for the hypothesis that stress is a positive factor in the progression of these illnesses. But, neither has it been proven that stress is not a major causative factor in any or all of these diseases. In fact it would seem that the medical and scientific communities are in some state of disagreement about this issue. So while many doctors and scientists remain unconvinced about the importance of the stress syndrome in many diseases including the ones which were previously listed, it might be concluded that:

> There can be little doubt about the negative impact of stress upon the body. Evidence has suggested that stress, at the very least, provides a serious complicating effect upon such illnesses as high blood pressure and heart disease. Many eminent physicians see the stress reaction in a far more serious light, as a root cause of illness, both physical and mental.

The high incidence of stress is very clearly mirrored within society itself. Dr. Harold Bloomfield[5] suggests the following statistics which indicate the complexity and magnitude of stress reactions in the United States. There are currently 230 million prescriptions written per year in our country. Of these are five billion doses of tranquilizers, three billion doses of amphetamines and five billion doses of barbiturates. These statistics, by the way, discount the use of nonprescription and/or illegal drugs. According to Bloomfield, the great majority of these dosages are written for the alleviation of fatigue, hypertension, and insomnia which just happen to be the primary symptoms of stress. He further suggests that half of all the deaths in the United States are linked to heart disease, that one third of all adult males in this country suffer from high blood pressure, that ten percent of American adults have a peptic ulcer, and that physicians are increasingly reporting that psychosomatic illness is their major health-care and treatment problem. These incredible statistics point to another and perhaps the most serious conclusion so far, that:

The number-one health problem in the United States today is stress.[6]

Dr. Benson cites the work of the late cardiologist Dr. Samuel Levine, which strongly supports Dr. Bloomfield's assertion that stress is our greatest national health problem. Levine made a study of heart disease within families that he followed for long periods of time. He pointed out that where fathers and sons were both stricken by heart disease, the average time of the first attack was thirteen years earlier for the son than it was for the father. This phenomenon may logically be taken to represent the dramatic increase of stress agents within our society. Or, in other words, the world that we live in has rapidly become a more dangerous place than we realized. Our sociotechnical systems have increased in complexity to the point where, like cigarettes, they are hazardous to our health.

Who Am I?

When I first began teaching graduate courses in human resources management, I devised a set of exercises whose basic purpose was to help students identify and deal with fundamental issues in human relations. My first lecture always stressed the importance of learning about oneself before moving off into the more comfortable exercises of interpreting interpersonal behavior. The first homework assignment was to take a mirror, look into it for a full five minutes, and then write a short essay entitled, "Who Am I?"

While this experience seemed simple at first, it was a powerful vehicle for focusing attention upon the complex problem of self-awareness. First reactions by the students who completed this exercise included an almost completely objective or removed examination of the image in the mirror. Students tended to view the "person" in the mirror as if he were a distinct individual. And they began to ask themselves unanswerable questions about that "person" and why he did the things he did. In most cases, the graduate students reported that this was, indeed, a very difficult and challenging assignment which taught them more about what they didn't know about who they were, than what they did know.

Each of us is a truly unique and complex entity. We exist and, of that, most of us feel confident. But beyond this fundamental assertion, most of us have some serious doubts concerning who we are. Man would appear to be such a complex array of biological and chemical and electrical and psychological and emotional components that it is not even possible for the greatest of scientists to explain the mystery of life. Where did we come from? Why are we here? Where are we going?

Nature and Complex Man

Most of us spend our entire lives running around like so many busy ants in a colony who do exactly what needs to be done in terms of work, according to the norms of the "anthill." Perhaps the greatest tragedy is that so little of our time is directed toward learning about ourselves. It remains true, however, that the average person gets so caught up in his day-to-day affairs that he loses sight of what life may be all about.

Perhaps the greatest explorations of the next few decades will not take place in space or below the seas but, rather, inside the human being. Inner space may become the last great frontier for discovery. It is obvious that each of us holds a great deal of untapped potential. But how can we begin to more fully explore our inner space? How can we expand the limits of our awareness?

A growing number of scientists are beginning to suggest that the door to inner space has been locked by stress. Conversely, the reduction of stress holds the key to all kinds of dramatic potentials for people. The next chapter will present the scientific evidence that surrounds the relationship between stress and human capacity. And, more specifically, it will present a technique for effectively dealing with this stress, and for beginning the systematic exploration of inner space.

chapter 5

The Science of Creative Intelligence

It might be best to begin this chapter with a summary of the logical progression which has been presented so far within the book. We began by viewing the world of work and the changes which have accompanied the past twenty to thirty years of technological progress. Next, we viewed the science of management and the ways in which modern organizational theory was able to predict problems at work. This led to Chapter 3 which included a discussion of the reasons why employees of all kinds of organizations are subjected to a great deal of stress. Finally, the last chapter explained what stress is, discussed how it manifests itself within a person, and also dealt with both the symptoms and the results of accumulated stresses.

What we have seen then, is a grim picture of highly stressed workers whose jobs increasingly place more and more demands upon their physical and psychological health. The end result is a national syndrome of stress symptoms such as high blood pressure and ulcers, which are partially masked by the concurrent social dilemmas of alcoholism and drug abuse. And perhaps the most urgent concern of all is that these problems could certainly get much worse before they get better!

But to those of us who have spent some time working at jobs and thinking about the impact of these jobs upon ourselves and others, these ideas are not really new. Many writers have recognized the problems of organizational life and tried to deal with anxiety at work. But there is no widely accepted solution for this dilemma of stress. Perhaps the most dangerous aspect of the entire problem is that the existence and dangers of job-related anxieties are virtually ignored by all of us. What happens then is that we very gradually immerse ourselves in our highly stressed worlds, training ourselves, in effect, to absorb without recognizing an ever-increasing barrage of stress. So, by the time most of us reach adulthood with its correlated problems and responsibilities, we have become highly stressed beings who are oblivious to our situations. If any of us were suddenly able to return to the kind of emotional and psychological state of the typical five-year-old, for example, we would surely note an overwhelming feeling of calmness and happiness and freedom. This dramatic transition would occur largely as the result of the dissolution of the stresses which we have accumulated over our lifetimes.

Since it is impossible to travel back to our childhood, even for effect, our approach to stress management must be very different. First we must become convinced that stress plays the major role in the disruption of our general health, and that it keeps us from reaching our full potential as creative human beings. Then we must seek a method or technique for resolving it.

Techniques Versus Theories

This is surely an age of science. Since almost all of us have been involved in a society which is focused upon the development and proof of scientific phenomena, we have completely accepted the scientific approach. If a phenomenon cannot be ordered within a body of science and verified, many of us simply refuse to accept it. Our skepticism is also multiplied by the many examples of false advertising, misleading claims, and unfair business practices that we have all experienced. But, as much as we depend upon science to help us with our problems, we also misunderstand the approaches and limitations of the scientific method.

Science is a systematic attempt to explain the realities of the world about us. Thus, taking first things first, there are many continuing phenomena in existence about the world and its most apparent creature, mankind. The method of science is simply attempting to learn about these phenomena through its systematic approaches. But the scientist is limited by his constrained understanding. He is trained in the theories which are popular within his field. He learns one or more of these, and then may spend an entire career trying to combine or to prove or to disprove certain aspects of this single theory.

Many of our greatest scientific advances, however, have come from relatively unscientific places. (Since science is the process of discovery, there surely is no such thing, strictly speaking, as an unscientific place.) Serendipity effects, accidents, or radical scientists would seem to have made many of our most important contributions.

Galileo, for example, was thought to be a kind of crazy person when he began to write about the "motion" of the stars and the position of the earth within a solar system within a galaxy. His great "mistake" according to the reputable scientists of the time was to abandon existing theory for a foolish method of observation and verification. When early European sailors first discovered the sloop rig which could be used to make a boat sail toward the direction of the wind rather than following the trade winds, they were accused of using magic and of being devil worshippers.

So, there has traditionally been quite a lot of resistance and "scientific" skepticism to new notions. This is particularly true of concepts which do not come from the center of existing and accepted theory. One of the finest examples of this process is the scientific and general skepticism which has associated itself with meditation.

Meditation, itself, is a very neutral and universal technique. It has continued to be a part of many Eastern and Western traditions for thousands of years. Yet it is a misunderstood and mysterious concept to most people. In the past, meditation has never been discussed or investigated in the kind of operational terms which could lead to scientific verification. That was because of the abundance of very complex approaches to teaching the practice of meditation.

Meditation and Tradition

The most obvious illustrations of our popular notion of meditation come from our understanding (or lack thereof) of Eastern tradition. Zen Buddhism includes a number of meditative practices. These are directed toward helping the person achieve a feeling of no feeling, or a state of nothingness. Taoism, the religion of China, includes an exercise where one is to achieve a tranquil state by concentrating on nothing. Japanese Shintoism also utilizes a kind of meditative technique which uses breathing exercises to achieve a state of tranquility. But perhaps the best-known examples of meditation, at least to those who live in the Western world, are the various yoga meditations which have become increasingly popular during the past few years. Again, these exercises are said to provide a feeling of calmness and inner strength.

The great majority of Americans, however, just cannot get beyond the problems which are connected with their image of meditation as a kind of mysterious Oriental technique. But these people simply don't understand the impact of meditative techniques upon Western culture and religion, or the fundamental relationship between Eastern and Western religion. Jesus was not born in New York City or, for that matter, in Europe. He was born in the tradition of Eastern culture. Thus, the religion which he generated has its basis in non-Western culture.

So this great and mysterious concept called *meditation* which conveys vague images of old guys wrapped in white sheets and running on hot rocks, has perhaps turned off many potential meditators. But, at the same time, the practice is so universal and fundamental to the cultures and religions of the past, that it needs to be re-evaluated in terms of our twentieth-century society.

A New Approach

Some years ago, a new teacher of a meditation technique appeared. Now it is not at all unusual for a new approach to emerge. Over the centuries there have undoubtedly been hundreds of thousands of approaches to meditation. But this particular technique was quite unique. And it was unique in terms of its simplicity. It would seem that in order to get into meditation in the past, one had to go through all kinds of complex intellectual and physical gyrations. Anyone who has had the experience of showing up for their local YMCA's annual course on meditation has heard these kinds of questions: "Have you read the Upanishads?" "Do you understand karma?" "Can you do the full lotus?" "Of course, you're a vegetarian, aren't you?" After about twenty minutes of this kind of dialogue, we are surely ready to run (not walk) home with a renewed resolution about not trying crazy things like that "meditation" course again. But this new approach to meditation, called *Transcendental Meditation (TM)*, was different. Instead of presenting another complex and mystical approach to the practice of meditation, Maharishi Mahesh Yogi developed and taught an Americanized technique. In fact this particular approach to meditation has caused the *Wall Street Journal* to refer to him as a latter-day "Dale Carnegie."[1]

Maharishi began his career as a student of physics in India. After receiving his degree, he studied for thirteen years with a teacher named Brahmananda Saraswati Shankaracharya of Jyotir Matr, who is said to be an expert in the ancient Vedic tradition of India. Following his study, he began work as a monk, teaching in India. In 1959, Maharishi shifted his concentration to the United States where the culture and times were evidently more amenable to his "simplistic and natural" approach.

Naturally, meditation is not taught for the sake of meditation itself. Perhaps it is this fact which has always been the complicating factor for Westerners. Traditional meditating techniques have always focused upon hard-to-swallow or mystical concepts such as cosmic consciousness or nirvana. While the Maharishi is every bit as interested in the ultimate aesthetics of meditation, or its capacity to allow man to evolve to higher and better forms, he has never pushed this aspect of TM. Instead he suggests that TM can simply help anyone to be a happier and more productive person. The technique can reduce stress, thus allowing one to become more efficient, less anxiety ridden, healthier, and more creative.

Perhaps it is this very simple and easy to understand introduction to the need to meditate, along with the overwhelming simplicity of the technique itself which has caused TM to be such an overwhelming success in the United States.

What Is TM?

First and foremost, TM is one of several meditative techniques. It has evolved, like other techniques, from the Vedic tradition of India. But unlike any other technique of meditation, TM is so simple and easy to learn that persons who utilize the technique can immediately experience many of the kinds of benefits which require years of practice with other approaches. Robert Wallace[2] has reported in his research that the changes in brain wave patterns among meditators, particularly the alpha waves which are taken to be an indication of relaxation or calmness, are similar to the measurements taken of Zen monks with twenty years or more experience. Measurements of the monks were taken by Drs. Kasamatsu and Hria,[3] Japanese physiologists.

Thus it might be said that the Maharishi has spent a lifetime developing and perfecting a technique for quickly learning how to meditate: a technique called Transcendental Meditation or TM.

Like many other techniques, TM utilizes a mantra, or pleasant sound. The meditator is trained in a few very simple lessons to understand what meditation is all about, how to go about the practice itself, and finally to recognize and use his personal mantra. The core of the TM technique is its mantra distribution system. Teachers of TM are trained to distribute mantras to individuals via six-month teacher-training courses which are held in different parts of the world. These teachers must have meditated for a number of years before they are allowed to apply for the teacher-training course.

Regarding the technique itself, meditators are told to practice TM for two twenty-minute periods daily. During these times, they are told to sit quietly in a relaxed position and to silently repeat their mantra. Once the technique has been learned it can be practiced with no additional training courses for an indefinite period. But teachers make what, in effect, consists of a lifetime commitment to their student meditators. They offer them help or advice about meditation whenever the need might arise. Advanced techniques are available for persons who have meditated for several years, but these are neither necessary nor pushed by the TM organization.

In essence, then, the Maharishi's approach consists of a very simple and natural mental technique which involves no religious or philosophical commitment, no organizational attachments nor special postures or diets. It is a simplified approach to relaxation.

Criticisms of TM

In the two years or so that I have spent eagerly scrounging through the literature of TM I have been overwhelmed at the general lack of negative kinds of articles. Fundamentally it can be said that there are few if any criticisms of the technique itself, or of the effects of the technique upon practitioners. I have also noted in my own research that the articles which are even semicritical in nature appear in the less professional journals. In other words, the more prestigious, professional, and scientific the treatment of TM, from an experimental viewpoint, the more positive the conclusions would seem to be.

However, in fairness to the work that has been done, I think that some reference should be made to the kinds of criticisms which have been identified with TM, and these seem to fall into three distrinct groups.

1. The secrecy of the mantra distribution technique
2. The organization which markets TM
3. The price of the training

Some people have been put off by the fact that the process or system by which mantras are distributed to individual meditators is a closely guarded secret. Meditators are told not to divulge their particular mantra to anyone, and the teachers of TM are consistent in their stock reply to the question, "where does my mantra come from?" From my own perspective the greatest single rebuttal of this criticism comes from the process of teacher training. At this time (and this figure is changing very rapidly) there are over 4,000 trained teachers of TM. These are persons who meditated for several years and then participated in a concentrated six-month training program (which requires a full six months of residence). These TM teachers represent a considerable cross section of humanity. I have personally met businessmen, career service people, graduate students, physicians, psychiatrists, old people, young people, men, and women who have been trained as TM teachers. And while many of them prefer to return to their occupations after training rather than working full-time at the job of teaching TM, all of them are fiercely loyal to both the technique and its master.

It would be hard for me, personally, to believe that if there were a shred of scientific doubt concerning the mantra distribution process, that one or more of the intelligent professional people who have learned it would have been heard from by now. Thus, I must assume, from their universal loyalty, that there is good justification for the secrecy of the mantra system, and that these teachers have learned what that justification is.

A second and perhaps more common complaint centers upon the International Meditation Society (IMS), the non-profit group which markets TM. It is said that this organization is a hopelessly inefficient model of any typical American company; and that this doesn't make any sense in terms of its mission which supposedly is to help mankind. My response to this criticism is mixed. First, I agree that the organization is not as efficient as it could be. But, like many other young organizations, it is naive in its approaches and has yet to learn from its own mistakes. It is also growing faster than any other young organization could comfortably expect to expand. It may be experiencing its own future shock. As regards the organization's form and approach, however, I feel that IMS has taken a sensible step. They hope to operate in a highly industrialized, marketing-oriented society, and thus must take a similar approach themselves if they hope to be effective.

Third and finally, more than a few persons have been put off by the cost of the training (which seems to be rising with the inflation of recent years). But there are a number of reasons for the fee, not the least of which involves the impact of the technique upon new meditators. It is not true only of the twentieth century that nobody gets "anything for nothing." That adage has been so universal throughout the history of the world that man has come to accept the fact that anything worth something costs something. Taken in another way, it might be said that anything which is simply given to you without cost (financial or otherwise) is automatically suspected of being not worthwhile. Thus the first, and perhaps primary, reason for charging a fee for TM is to insure that the person who learns TM has given up (or paid) something in exchange for his learning. This helps the meditator to place a higher value upon the technique as it is presented. Secondly, the fee, which is nominal in terms of the services offered, is used to secure the continued existence and growth of TM. And, looking from the perspective of the Maharishi, if the TM technique is truly as powerful as he is suggesting, then this is quite possibly a very valid application of the money which is collected. Some part of it, of course, pays for the livelihood of the TM teacher, but for the most part these and the other persons who work for IMS exist at a subsistence level in terms of wages. The Maharishi himself is a monk. He owns nothing, and collects no salary. The organization is incorporated as a nonprofit educational organization and its financial statements are open to the public.

In summary then, there would seem to be few if any generic criticisms of TM. None of the professional journals which have addressed specific technical issues relative to TM have made any kinds of negative assertions about the technique. This, in itself, is quite remarkable considering the extent of the research which has explored the various impacts of TM.

The Growth of TM

There have been many techniques or approaches to meditation which have been brought to the United States during the past several years. But perhaps the most apparent characteristic of TM which sets it apart from other approaches has been its phenomenal growth. Unlike other methods of meditation which appear to catch on for a short period of time, become popular, and then fizzle out, TM appears to be experiencing a steady and increasing growth rate.

In the early sixties when the Maharishi first began to teach Transcendental Meditation, it was the rare person who had even heard of TM. The early years of TM were also spotted by the notoriety of some of the more famous meditators. The Beatles, The Beach Boys, and Mia Farrow were among the Maharishi's best-known clients. Many feel that this early notoriety which came from the Maharishi's associations with celebrities did not help the credibility of TM. But others, who are perhaps more astute, point not only to the instant advertising which came as a result of famous meditators, but to the positive influence which can be seen in the lives of some of the more public figures which were initiated. Close followers of the Beatles, for example, will note a very radical change from a kind of raucus and confused group of young men who were involved in all kinds of marginally productive activities, such as drug abuse and the rock "groupie" scene, to a more mellow and certainly more musically competent group. Finally the

Beatles evolved from a typical teen-age rock band to become individually well-respected composers and performers.

The latest statistics[4] suggest that there are 2,400 trained teachers in this country and another 1,600 elsewhere. These teachers are training an average of 10,000 new meditators per month. This growth can be appreciated in terms of the 1965 estimate which suggested that there were a total of 200 active meditators. This phenomenal growth is clearly being facilitated by the acceptance of TM in many school systems. Many primary and secondary schools have adopted courses in "The Science of Creative Intelligence" as part of their regular curricula. Francis Driscoll, Superintendent of Eastchester, New York, schools reports that SCI courses are a great success within his system. His experiences suggest that TM causes students to:

1. Improve their grades
2. Get along with their teachers
3. Accept their parents
4. Get along with other students
5. Reduce the use of drugs

Another interesting transition within the past few years of TM's growth has been the increased acceptance of the technique among older people. At first, and perhaps because of Maharishi's associations with people like the Beatles, TM had its greatest appeal on the college campus. Most of the initiates seemed to be in their late teens or early twenties. But lately that trend has begun to reverse itself. William Witherspoon, a regional coordinator with IMS, reported to me that the average age of new meditators has passed the magical "thirty" mark and is rapidly moving toward "forty." In addition, the classic question which used to be, "I like TM so much but how can I convince my mother and father to try it?" has reversed. Now it is, "How can I get my children interested in TM?"

Meditation and Science

Perhaps the most important reason for the growth of TM lies in the fact that the technique has scientific credibility. It would seem that whenever a new thing like TM emerges in our society, making claims which border upon the medical, psychological, sociological, educational, and management communities, individuals within the research disciplines quickly attempt to test the assertions which have been made. Many times the scientific evidence helps to support the technique and to suggest new kinds of diagnostic applications. Programs are underway at this time, for example, in prisons, school systems, mental-health clinics, psychiatric institutions, drug-abuse centers, alcoholism-treatment facilities, and, last but not least, business firms.

The remainder of this chapter will be devoted to a treatment of some of the scientific evidence which has emerged regarding TM and the impact of the technique upon the person.

Early Research

It would seem that there are always a few pioneer researchers in a given field. In the area of TM, the two names which constantly and recurrently emerge are Benson and Wallace. Dr. Wallace presented a Ph.D. thesis at the University of California Department of Physiology that was perhaps the first sophisticated piece of research done on TM. Dr. Benson, from the Harvard Medical School, began reporting some of his own research shortly after that time. Between these two scientists, who have now co-authored a number of studies of TM and stress, there have been close to a dozen significant research publications in such prestigious journals as *Scientific American*, *The American Journal of Physiology*, *Science*, and *The New England Journal of Medicine*. Their studies proved important in the introduction of TM to both the scientific and medical communities. In addition, they paved the way for hundreds of additional research projects and diagnostic programs that followed.

Wallace's first study, "The Physiological Effects of TM,"[5] focused upon several different physiological measurements of meditators which were taken before, during, and after meditation. A sample of fifteen normal college students who had practiced TM for time periods ranging from one-half to three years was randomly selected for the experiment. The experiment itself attempted to measure changes in oxygen consumption, heart rate, skin resistance, and brain-wave patterns during TM. It was found in this pioneering study that, during TM, oxygen consumption decreased, the heart slowed appreciably, skin resistance increased, and brain-wave patterns changed significantly. The conclusion to this first study was many faceted. First and foremost, TM seemed to cause a specific set of responses within the body. Second, and on the basis of reduced oxygen consumption, heart rate, and changes in skin resistance, it was determined that the changes appeared to be in the direction of calmness, tranquility, or the reduction of the stress syndrome. Thirdly, the brain-wave patterns which were experienced as a result of TM were found to be uniquely different from other known brain-wave patterns. The indication was, then, that TM was generically different from sleep, hypnosis, or other known mental states.

Benson's first study appeared in the 1969 *New England Journal of Medicine.*[6] It was entitled "Yoga for Drug Abuse." In this short article, Dr. Benson simply noted the fact that experimental volunteers had reported an increasing distaste for drug experiences due to their increased involvement with TM. Benson further suggested that TM might be a very fruitful area for future research.

Evidently Benson took his own advice, for in 1972 he and Dr. Wallace co-authored perhaps the classic research effort in TM and physiology, "The Physiology of Meditation," which appeared in *Scientific American,*[7] a widely read and highly reputable journal. Thirty-six meditators took part in a study in two different locations—Boston City Hospital and The University of California at Irvine. Following is a list of the conclusions suggested by their study.

The metabolic rate as measured by oxygen consumption and carbon dioxide elimination was decreased significantly during meditation. Subjects experienced an immediate reduction in the rate of oxygen consumption as a result of TM. This was taken by the researchers to indicate a unique state of relaxation. They also reported that metabolic rest associated with TM was much deeper than the changes associated with sleep.

Circulatory changes were also noted within the meditating group. First, blood pressure fell to a systolic reading of 106 and diastolic pressure of 57 during the premeditation period. This reduction of blood pressure persisted throughout the experimental period. In other words, TM was accompanied by a constant but low blood pressure. Perhaps more interesting was the fact that blood lactate levels declined greatly during the meditative period. Lactate, which is caused by the anaerobic metabolism, is usually taken to represent a high level of anxiety, neurosis, or high blood pressure. While some lactate is almost always dissolved during rest, Benson and Wallace found that blood lactate dissipated three times faster during TM. They concluded that TM must affect the sympathetic nerve network. It was this particular finding which positively linked TM with the treatment of hypertension.

Wallace and Benson concluded that TM might well provide a counterresponse to the fight-or-flight reflex. They state that:

> The pattern of changes suggests that meditation generates an integrated response, or reflex, that is mediated by the central nervous system. A well-known reflex of nature was described by Harvard psychologist, Walter B. Cannon; it is called the "fight-or-flight" or "defense-alarm" reaction. The aroused sympathetic nervous system mobilizes a set of physiological responses marked by increases in the blood pressure, heart rate, blood flow to the muscles, and oxygen consumption. The hypometabolic state produced by meditation is, of course, opposite to this in almost all respects. It looks very much like a counterpart of the fight-or-flight reaction.[8]

Wallace and Benson also proposed the nature of the fight-or-flight reaction as a part of a national stress syndrome:

> During man's early history the defense-alarm system may well have had high survival values and thus have become strongly established in his genetic makeup. It continues to be aroused in all its

visceral aspects when the individual feels threatened. Yet in the environment of our time the reaction is often an anachronism. Although the defense-alarm reaction is generally no longer appropriate, the visceral response is evoked with considerable frequency by the rapid and unsettling changes that are buffeting modern society. There is good reason to believe the changing environment's incessant stimulations of the sympathetic nervous system are largely responsible for the high incidence of hypertension and similar serious diseases that are prevalent in our society.[9]

As founding fathers of a research discipline, Benson and Wallace did the scientifically difficult job of paving the way for new research. Their early studies suggested many new and important avenues for TM-related research.

TM and Cardiovascular Health

With the incredible incidence of heart disease in our society, a natural arena for TM research was the relationship between meditation and cardiovascular health. While the early studies of Benson and Wallace clearly suggested a strong positive relationship, much more research was needed in order to reach any solid conclusions.

An additional study by Wallace, Benson, and Wilson,[10] further supported the early findings that TM reduced both the heart rate and the oxygen-consumption rate. More importantly, however, this study also suggested the permanent and increasing nature of the benefits of meditation. In short, TM did not simply provide positive results during meditation. Meditation caused an instant decrease in both measures thus reducing the load on the entire cardiovascular system, but it also resulted in heart and breath rates which remained lower than before meditation, even after the meditation period ended. In addition, meditators were found to have significantly lower than average blood pressures.

In a study of respiratory therapy, Honsberger and Wilson[11] found that TM was useful in the treatment of asthma. The researchers hypothesized that since TM reduced oxygen consumption, then it might reduce the symptoms of asthma, hypoexemia, or the lack of oxygen. Using a treatment group over a six-month period it was found that 94 percent of the asthmatic meditators reported improvements in their symptoms. It was concluded that TM relaxed the respiratory system thus reducing the airway resistance usually associated with asthma.

Allison[12] reports significant reductions in respiration as a result of TM. He observed that respiratory rate fell from about 14 per minute to about 6 per minute almost immediately, and then to about 4 per minute toward the end of the meditative period. Following TM, the rate rose again, but not to the point where it had been before. Using other approaches, Allison found that he could not elicit the kind of change or deep rest which resulted from TM by using any other known technique for relaxation.

In 1972, Benson and Wallace[13] reported the result of a direct attempt to lower the blood pressures of hypertensive patients at the Harvard Medical School. While the twenty-two subjects continued their normal treatments, control measures showed that TM had successfully reduced their average blood pressure from 150 systolic and 94 diastolic to 141 and 88 respectively.

Although the evidence is not all in yet, and the number of research projects dealing with TM and cardiovascular function is rapidly growing, the early indications are that TM shows great promise for fighting heart disease. The technique appears to induce deep rest and to help the body achieve a more healthy and vigorous state. Studies have demonstrated that TM helps the body's entire cardiovascular system to operate more efficiently, thus reducing the load and the wear and tear on the heart.

TM and Psychological Health

The literature on TM and the psychology or mental health of the meditator is even more profuse than the literature dealing with cardiovasular disease. Perhaps this is because of the inherent relationship between TM and mental process.

Some of the early studies which dealt with specific electromechanical processes of the brain were perhaps too technical to be of general interest. But, these have now been joined by studies which are oriented more particularly toward behavior patterns and toward success within particular situations.

Brown, Stewart and Blodgett[14] were among the first to report the physical changes in brain functioning as a result of TM. Using an experimental group of eleven meditators and a control group of eleven nonmeditators, the researchers attempted to measure the impact of TM upon brain-wave functioning. They found that meditation was, in fact, accompanied by some rather unique brain-wave patterns which they called kappa-rhythm activity. They conclude that TM is a unique state of consciousness, and not simply a semisleep kind of state. Further, they suggest that EEG data support the possibility that meditation is a "higher" level of mental activity.

Banquet[15] also studied the impact of TM upon EEG functions. Using ten subjects he measured changes in the frequency, form, and amplitude of brain waves. These were the same kinds of changes which Wallace, Benson, and Wilson noted in their research. Wallace et al. referred to the altered brain-wave patterns as *a state of restful inner alertness!*

Stimulated by the clear indications of a relationship between TM and brain activity, a number of researchers addressed themselves to the various implications of TM upon psychological functions.

Orme-Johnson[16] used galvanic skin response, an electrical measure of skin resistance, to measure the stability of the nervous system. He measured the GSR of meditators and nonmeditators, and concluded that TM acts to stabilize the nervous system as indicated by the presence of fewer galvanic skin responses by meditators. He also found that the improved stability was present after the period of meditation. Orme-Johnson suggested that:

1. TM strengthens the individual's nervous system.

2. Meditators recover more quickly from stress.

3. TM also develops a more stable pattern of responses to stressful situations.

4. Efficiency in the nervous system allows the energy to be used for more purposeful activity.

Nidich, Seeman, and Siebert[17] investigated the relationship between TM and anxiety. Using a psychological instrument to measure state anxiety they found that while there was no difference between the TM and control groups before TM training, six months after training the TM group scored significantly lower on the anxiety scale when confronted with a demanding task.

Hjelle[18] has studied the impact of TM upon anxiety, self-control and self-actualization. He measured twenty-one new meditators on the Bendig (anxiety), the Rotter (control), and Shostrom (self-actualization) scales. The results showed experienced meditators to be less anxious, more internally controlled, and more self-actualized than the novice group. This is one of the few research projects which has investigated the impact of the meditating experience. And its conclusions support the hypothesis that meditators not only enjoy more efficient psychological processes than nonmeditators, but that these benefits accrue over time.

Other psychologists have investigated the relationship between TM and a number of traditional personality characteristics. Results of the preliminary research efforts suggest that TM is positively linked to the reduction of depression, and the reduction of neuroticism. These studies, taken as a group, indicate that TM is strongly related to psychological health, and also that the extent of the emotional well-being which is associated with TM is related to the length of meditating experience.

Therapeutic Applications

The acceptance of TM in some scientific areas has been so enthusiastic that a number of people have embarked upon programs where TM has been applied to specific problems.

Perhaps the best known of these areas is the problem of drug abuse. Since TM helps to normalize or stabilize psychological health, it was reasoned that the application of TM might remove the need for drugs, thus reducing drug dependency. This relationship between TM and drug abuse has emerged as perhaps the most prolific single area of study. Another logical area of application is in the treatment of alcoholism. Researchers have found that meditators report significant reductions in the use of prescription drugs, nonprescription drugs, and even the social drugs such as alcohol, and cigarettes.

A second and rapidly increasing application of TM is the criminal justice system. Early indications are that TM may provide a much needed normalizing effect upon prisoners, thus neutralizing the stresses and strains of prison routines. Perhaps TM can ultimately provide some useful tools for reclaiming these forgotten members of our society.

TM has also become a tool of several school systems. While this particular application may interact with the drug abuse problem, many school administrators are very excited about the potential of TM for facilitating not only learning but socialization within school curricula.

Beyond the Technique

Proponents of TM market the practice itself as a very simple, easy-to-understand, easy-to-learn, and natural process. They are most careful to emphasize the fact that TM is not a religion or a philosophy. And it is clear that, in terms of the mechanics of the practice and the process of learning, TM is essentially a neutral kind of process. Many religious persons (priests, nuns, and ministers) have learned to meditate with very pleasing results. But beyond the simple salesmanship, it is also obvious that TM is a very powerful personal experience which has the potential to make meaningful and significant changes in a person. But, what are these changes, and do they not, in fact, confound our religious beliefs?

To begin with the changes, TM is said to reduce stress. So we might simply expect that a meditator would be a person whose stress had been lowered. But the real meaning of this reduced stress is magnified by two very important principles:

1. TM is said to have an aggregate beneficial effect upon a person.

2. Modern society is a source of incredibly great stress.

The broad implication, then, is that since we are a nation or perhaps a race of very highly stressed beings, then the reduction of this stress is likely to affect us in a very powerful way. And this brings us back to the original question of religion. What is religion? How is it that a technique which affects us in a fundamental way could not somehow affect our religious nature if it is to bring about powerful changes via the systematic resolution of stress?

Perhaps the answers to these questions lie in part of the discussions of meditation which were presented earlier in the chapter. While meditation, the technique, is not particular to any kind of religious experience, the notion of meditation is inherent in almost every major religion. The religions of the world have always sought a development of the whole man. So perhaps TM, accidentally on the part of the meditator and by design from the position of its designer, interacts with the religious experience (taken in a very broad context) to help man develop himself.

I can well imagine that anyone who reads the preceding paragraph will begin to wonder if TM could do some kind of harm to his personal religious experience. Many persons who approach TM are frightened or put off by what they regard as religious overtones. Such questions as "Can I practice TM and still be a Catholic (or Lutheran or Methodist or Jew?") are not uncommon. This is probably the fundamental reason why TM is marketed as *not* being a religion or a philosophy.

But the fact remains that TM, if we are to accept the scientific evidence, has a powerful effect upon the practitioner. Thus, if religion deals with the whole man and his ultimate development *TM must be an integral part of religion and religious experience.*

But it is also just as clear to those who have investigated the technique from the perspective of theology that *TM enhances the religious experience. It does not replace any particular set of beliefs. Thus TM can be a part of any religion.*

To support this position I have taken the time to discuss the problem of TM and religion with the Director of Graduate Studies in Theology at Gannon, Dr. (Rev.) Robert Levis. He noted the existence of the mantra concept in the Christian tradition, and particularly within the Eastern rites of Christianity. With his help I was able to locate a work entitled *Christian Yoga*[19] by J.M. Dechanet. Dechanet discusses the long evolution of meditative experience including the use of mantras (as used in TM) within Christianity. He speaks of early and pure forms of Christian prayer which involved the use of single syllables or sets of sounds rather than long groups of words with complex semantic meanings.

One tradition in particular was "The Prayer of Jesus" in which a person learned to pronounce the word *Jesus* to himself over and over again simultaneously using breath control. The user would utter the first syllable as he inhaled and the second as he exhaled. Monology was another common contemplative approach used by early Christian monks. It was said that prayers should not consist of great notes or flowing expressions, but that one word is enough to "touch the Father in heaven."

Dechanet suggests that the practice of yoga (meaning meditation) can help us to

establish ourselves at the center of a true Christianity. As for the practices of Yoga, we shall take them simply for what they are, neither religion nor mysticism, but a discipline, a skill admittedly ingenious. It is the art of uniting, of gathering together in man the elements that are too often scattered or sundered; the art of bringing the life of the spirit to open out in him, this life that is more divine for the Christian than for the Hindu. It is the art of joining, of helping grace to unite with God, his privileged creature, and this belongs to Christian Yoga alone. For us, Yoga shall be the technique that allows man, when this is fitting, to establish himself in silence; not merely away from noise, but effectively in the silence of the senses, desires and human passions. In the silence of mind, banishing preoccupying thoughts and worries, accepting above all to remain silent so that the Holy Spirit of God may now and then make its voice heard, and the spirit of the man may be listening.[20]

Clearly, then, meditation in the broadest sense is not foreign to the Western or Christian or Jewish traditions which form our socioreligious environments. And TM, taken as a highly efficient form of meditation, does not confound or interfere with any particular religious belief. It is surely a part of religious experience, but then possibly no more than any other particular activity which we might engage in. Perhaps, for example, going to college to become educated might be interpreted, at least in the broad sense, as enhancing our religious experience.

Self-Actualized Man

At this point it would seem appropriate to bring the "Science of Creative Intelligence" as it has been presented so far, with its various discussions of meditation, religion, and other unfamiliar language, together with some more practical or business-oriented language. And perhaps the one man who has added the most in this particular area is Abraham Maslow,[21] who has contributed the notion of a need hierarchy.

Maslow suggests that each of us has several different kinds of motivational needs, and that these fall into five ascending categories:

1. Simple survival needs, such as safety, security, proper temperature, shelter, a pleasant environment

2. Social needs, meaning the continued assurance of strong affiliation bonds, friendships, family ties

3. Self-esteem needs, which reassure us that we are useful and worthwhile persons who are respected for our integrity

4. Needs for autonomy, which reinforce our own feelings of independence or individuality

5. Self-actualizing, meaning a state of positive and high awareness which is typified by a great deal of love in terms of

relationships, and a very high level of effectiveness in terms of activity

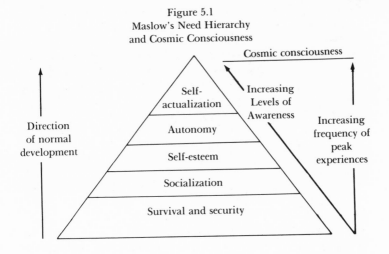

Figure 5.1
Maslow's Need Hierarchy
and Cosmic Consciousness

Maslow sees these needs as arranged in a kind of hierarchical order (Figure 5.1) with lower-order needs at the base of the triangle, and higher-order needs toward the top. In his view of development, a person begins at the bottom and proceeds through the need profile toward the top. If nothing impedes the progress of this normal human development, each person has an equal opportunity to become fully self-actualized.

A normal scheme might begin at a very early age with the young child who becomes immersed in life with little or no understanding of what this strange process is all about. His first needs are to secure a steady flow of basic things such as food, shelter, clothing, and safety. Thus, for his first several years he may show a great deal of concern for one or more of these lower-order needs. He is afraid of the dark and he can't go to sleep. Or he is concerned that he won't get enough to eat. But then he gradually turns his attention away from first-level things and toward the next higher level in the need hierarchy.

He becomes concerned about establishing and maintaining friendships, for example.

It is in this way that each person embarks upon a life of increasing awareness and development, moving from level to level toward the realization of self-actualization. But each time we enter a unique situation, for example, a new job, we can be jarred back into an awareness of lower-level needs. If a man is hungry, how can you expect him to work well? That person, motivated by the reality of hunger (which is a lower-order need) will react by displacing his attentions from higher needs toward the fulfillment of his lowest unsatisfied need—hunger.

And there lies the fundamental reason why so few of us attain the highest possible levels of actualization. It would seem that every time our lives become so well ordered that we can begin to focus in on real progress toward a higher level of needs, something changes to rattle the skeletons of our previously fulfilled (and lower order) needs.

Just as a manager begins to feel that he is making great progress in terms of his self-concept, and that he might begin to move on toward higher-order autonomy needs, some interpersonal catastrophe strikes at the job and he begins to re-evaluate and question the prior resolution of his social needs. Thus the whole flow of systematic progress is broken, perhaps leaving permanent scars, so that redirection toward self-actualization becomes more and more difficult.

Maslow's work sadly suggests that very few of us ever make significant progress in terms of self-actualization. We spend most of our time vacillating between several of the middle levels of development. In fact, many of us probably do not make much progress beyond the lower-level needs. He views this as both the fault and the loss of the complex technical systems within which we work. The large organizations are so product- or system-goal-oriented that they fail to appeal to the continuing complex needs of their participants.

But somehow some of us seem to escape this constant fragmentation of motivational progression. And when this unique individual, an Einstein or a Galileo or an Edison or a

Whitman, becomes visible to the rest of us, their superior work and their maneuvered capacity to understand reality is so incredibly superior that all of us are drawn to it. We view the output of these select few persons, and we reason that they must be lucky geniuses, a sort of elite few who are as far removed from our own potential as possible.

But could this view be a kind of cop-out on our part? I wonder if it is not a defense mechanism, which while protecting us from the ultimate reality of failure, may also impede our own personal development?

The Psychology of Peak Experiences

Each of us has found that while his life proceeds in a more or less orderly way, there are some days or mornings or moments which are very different from others. These times, both highs and lows, can be interpreted in two substantially different ways.

The first view is that the human condition is simply a series of cycling emotional, mental, and physical feelings. There are some very high days, followed by many average or middle days, and then some very low days. Each of us is simply a victim of these natural cycles and must resign himself or herself to this relatively natural course of events.

There is substantial evidence, however, to support a much different point of view. After all, how do we account for not only the cycles within an individual but also the fact that some persons are perpetually more enthusiastic, healthy, and vigorous than others, or that through counseling, psychoanalysis, or chemotherapy, some perennially low or depressed persons make visible progress toward a more healthy and vigorous state.

Perhaps the natural state of a person is a state which is associated with high levels of mental and emotional enthusiasm and physical vigor. Then the existence of these differences between and within persons is a simple and natural illustration of our great potential for progress.

Peak experiences, whether they are highs or lows, may be

viewed from this second perspective as important learning tools. Each of us can probably recall one or more such days within his immediate past. It is a highly unique and personal kind of phenomenon. Perhaps we wake up one morning feeling like a "tiger." We are refreshed, invigorated, and happy. It is probable that everything we do that day will turn out just a little bit better. Perhaps our peak experience is associated with a vacation or an achievement or with another person. In any event, we can almost universally agree about the existence of these phenomena.

If we are to learn from these peaks, we should know what they illustrate and how this information can be of use in our jobs or our everyday lives. There is every reason to believe that our highs and our lows show us the path toward personal progress. The very good days are indications of where we could go in terms of our overall creative potential. The very bad days may be illustrations of where we have been.

It would follow in logic, then, that as we begin to experience more and more peak-experience days, that these peaks gradually replace the norm of "lower" days and soon we are experiencing "superpeak experiences" in respect to our prior position. In this way progress toward self-actualization can be understood by the great majority of us who are still bouncing around in the cellar of the need-hierarchy. We must seize upon some technique which encourages us to progress. We must try to make yesterday's highs tomorrow's lows!

What this means in terms of practical reality is so clear that we hardly need to articulate it. Perhaps our greatest detriment is our failure to use our fullest potential. I can see an illustration of this within my own students. As class after class of graduate students (future administrators and managers of corporate America) pass through the portals of my own college (Gannon's MBA program), I hear a kind of universal set of hopes and aspirations. Graduating MBA's tell me that they want to be very successful at their jobs and careers. They have very high professional ideals and goals—to become presidents, vice-presidents and board chairmen. Yet at the same time they express concerns for their families. They want good positive relationships with their spouses and children. They need to develop solid and balanced families filled with activities which are mutually rewarding for the entire family. But these young men and women are very concerned about their capacity to do both things simultaneously. Many hedge their strategem. "I will give up just enough of my personal and family attentions to be moderately successful." "I will be a company man only to a point, then, if necessary, I will opt for a somewhat less glamorous career." In short, they see a kind of impending choice: work versus family!

But what if each of those MBA graduates could anticipate that even his worst days, his least productive ones, would be the kind of peak experience days where we charge off in the morning ready to wrestle with a bear. Then they could put aside their concerns about the conflict of values between career and family. They would be able to do an outstanding job of both, with time left over for other activities. This is the picture of Maslow's self-actualized man; a highly developed and efficient person whose accomplishments are both balanced and fruitful.

The question which remains is a very simple one. How do we get that way? What should we do? What is the "magic" secret for this kind of personal evolution?

The Burden of Stress

To answer the dilemma of what is holding us back we need simply refer to the prior chapters of this book. Living in a highly stressed social and technical environment we find that as our levels of stress increase, the capacity to be enthusiastic, vigorous, energetic, and efficient falls dramatically. Selye's work suggested that stresses are absorbed on a daily basis and then stored within the body in the form of chemical scars. This intake and aggregation of stresses reduces our overall ability to react productively within situations because it requires the increasing utilization of our internal mechanisms to fight the stresses.

Selye's model includes two kinds of stress—distress and eustress. Eustress is the kind of phenomenon within our collective environment which elicits a specific reaction by the body. *Distress* which would be synonymous with the general term *stress* as we have discussed it, is a generically different kind of phenomenon. While it comes from the same basic environment where we find eustress, distress engages a sequence of nonspecific responses within us.

To clarify this, the weightlifter places a specific stress upon a muscle. The body makes a specific integrated response to this demand thus coping nicely with eustress. Or an engineer is faced with a deadline which he feels that he can make. He utilizes his skills as an engineer to complete his work on time. These examples are not to be confused with stress or distress in terms of Seyle's work. These and many other eustresses are not stresses and thus do not eat away at us as distresses do.

But a great definitional difficulty arises in the application of these concepts to real-life situations. Whenever I talk about stress to a group of managers, for example, someone will invariably raise his hand and ask the following question: Isn't some stress necessary in business? After all, if there were no pressures, who would do anything?

The answer to this question is clear, but not an easy one to explain. The trick, here, lies within the subtle differences between individuals and their reactions to things. It is entirely possible that eustress, for one individual, would be distress for another. Let's use the jogger as an illustration. A person who has jogged steadily for several years faces the daily eustress of moving his body three or four miles at a relatively rapid pace. But the body has adapted itself to this task and has developed a specific mechanical response pattern. As a result, the jogger is, in some respects, better adapted to the general stress of running. But if we were to ask a sedentary individual to run for three or four miles, his or her body could become highly distressed by the experience. That running could, in fact, damage a person who had not entered a specific adaptation program which was oriented toward running.

Turning toward the more realistic problems of the working world, we find the same basic kind of phenomena. Different people take greatly diverse approaches to their jobs. So a single phenomenon in the work environment such as "time pressure" can elicit different reactions among various persons. For one man, time pressure may be a stress, but for another, it is not. For most persons the picture is even more complicated, however. Pressure may largely be a comfortable or stimulating eustress with some resultant distress.

So the answer to my universal businessman's question is this, "It depends!" It depends upon what you mean by pressure. And it depends upon the individual. And it depends upon the approach of the boss.

Let's use this common experience of time pressure for an illustration. Everyone has probably faced the problem of a deadline. But each of us reacts in a very different way. Highly achievement-oriented people, for example, may react in various ways to time pressure on the basis of who initiates the goal. The high-achievement type likes to set his own goals in a moderately difficult framework, and then to accomplish them very successfully, In short, he sets easily attainable goals. Thus, if the boss tells a high-achievement type, "Have this done by tomorrow," he is more than likely to experience a good deal of stress since achievement-oriented persons have a strong need to be involved in the goal-setting process. Now if the task had been approached in a different way, the output might have been very different. If, for instance, the boss had asked the employee, "When can you have this done?" and the employee answered, "Tomorrow!" then chances are that the new self-imposed deadline (pressure) would not have caused any stress for the employee.

In this light, then, we can see that the stress-at-work issue is a very personal one. Some persons can plunge into what would seem to be a very stressful situation and excel. This is surely due to the fact that that particular kind of situation must match the needs of these particular individuals. Other persons placed in the very same situation would suffer the effects of great stress.

The Management of Stress

So what is one to do? If we are to make an attempt to alleviate stress for ourselves or for those who work around us we must enter into a supercomplex analysis of not only the individuals (including ourselves) who are in a working situation, but also of the environment itself. There are two very simple reasons which make such a strategy impractical if not impossible:

1. Individuals are both supercomplex and dynamic.

2. Work environments are both supercomplex and dynamic.

In practice, then, those of us who have spent much time or effort trying to intellectualize our way through the stress-management problem find that just as we think that we are beginning to understand something, the whole thing changes violently. And the most typical reaction is to give up or to ignore the whole problem.

A renewed understanding of the implied dangers of accumulated stress should suggest that each of us begin to concern himself with stress management. First we must insure our own continued growth, development, and our productivity at work. Next, we might attempt to unfold the full potential of our fellow workers, our coworkers as well as our subordinates. To avoid the continuing intellectual and analytical dilemma of what to do and how to do it we might seek a simple and proven technique such as TM and apply it to the work environment. And if TM is a powerful stress-reducing technique, as has been suggested by the research evidence presented earlier, then the overall outcome of TM ought to be more productive, happy, and vigorous employees. And if that is true then the solution to the management-of-stress question is quite clear. But is that true? What evidence is there to support the supposition that TM is related to productivity? These are the questions which will be explored in the following chapter.

part 3
Productivity and Stress

chapter 6
Meditators at Work

The purpose of this chapter is to introduce the actual studies of TM at work. We have seen the evolution of management practice and its impact upon the worker. We have also looked at stress, the causes, the results, and the positive technique of TM which is useful for reducing the level of aggregate stress in a person. But the pragmatic or even skeptical among us must still harbor some very serious doubts especially concerning TM and work. Can stress really cause a person to be less effective at his job? What proof can be presented for the proposition that TM or any other stress-reducing technique might increase productivity? And further, what, if any, effects could TM have upon job performance? These are the questions which will be addressed within this chapter. A study will be presented which asks some very basic questions. How does stress reduction affect work-oriented variables such as productivity, job satisfaction, turnover, interpersonal relations, and ambition? This first study will focus upon changes that take place in the job performance of persons who meditate. A second study, which will also be presented in this chapter, is directed toward the differences between meditators and nonmeditators at work. These two studies taken together provide a varied and systematic view of the impact of stress at work.

While this chapter will deal only with TM and the impact of that particular technique upon productivity variables, it is the logical assumption of this and following chapters that TM serves as a proxy for stress reduction. That is, as TM is introduced, the aggregate level of stress within individuals is reduced. There would seem to be ample evidence from the physiological literature in the preceding chapter to substantiate this position.

Meditating and the Scientific Community

Recently, I have run into scientific studies supporting the relationship between prayer and plant growth, the possibility of studying the human aura to find acupuncture points, and the power of parapsychological phenomena. In discussing with my associates these and other issues which obviously lie on the horizons of various research disciplines, I have encountered more than the usual amount of resistance. It would seem that even the most professionally oriented researchers are reluctant to accept the potential of phenomena which they cannot order within their own experience.

But just as surely as the motor car, the airplane, the telephone, the television, and other mysterious technical "improbabilities" have become integrated components of our society, many new phenomena (some incomprehensible in terms of our current conceptions of reality) will assume vital positions in our future lives.

Probably the last people to accept the potential of these new ideas, however, are the various members of the scientific community. These researchers are particularly skeptical and methodical in their approach to recognizing and legitimatizing new knowledge. And perhaps the most skeptical of all researchers are those who deal with management and organization behavior. So while research was proceeding at a rapid pace in the areas of physiology and medicine, neither the business community, nor the researchers in that area were paying any attention to the possible impact of TM upon work.

Strangely enough, however, a great deal of research was under way regarding stress. Most of this work was from an entirely different perspective than the simple and relatively easy-to-learn TM technique. It was highly theoretical and intellectual in orientation rather than experiential.

Early Research into TM and Business

The first overtures toward business applicability were made by the members of SIMS,[1] the TM organization. From their perspective it was entirely logical that the technique would greatly benefit productivity and other job-related performance variables. They were also armed with firsthand reports by working meditators who claimed to have experienced dramatic improvements at work. Thus, even at the beginning of the TM movement, teachers as well as practitioners spoke of the on-the-job benefits.

But this kind of testimonial evidence was not enough to light any fires under the business community or the management-oriented research community. So, for the most part, TM did not find itself in the limelight. However, as physiological, biological, psychological, and medical research grew both in volume and sophistication, many parts of the various studies undertaken in these fields began to overlap the areas which are of interest to managers. Thus, it was primarily this early nonmanagement research which began to kindle the fires of interest within some segments of the management community.

Bladsdell,[2] for example, studied the relationship between TM and dexterity in a study which was published in 1971. He found that meditators were able to perform both faster and more accurately than nonmeditators at complex tasks. Abrams[3] investigated learning ability which has been linked with problem-solving ability, particularly for complex work situations. He not only found that meditators were superior learners, but that as the length of experience with meditation increased, learning ability continued to improve.

Research has also suggested that TM improves reaction time. In fact, a number of professional athletes including Joe Namath, quarterback for the New York Jets, and Bill Walton, former center for the UCLA basketball team, have been drawn to TM. The research of Shaw and Kolb[4] showed that the practice of TM improved reaction time, increased alertness, reduced dullness, and improved physical efficiency. In their study they found that meditators' reaction times were superior to those of nonmeditators. They also found that for meditators, reaction time was better after the practice of TM than before.

Ferguson and Gowan[5] studied the relationship between TM and self-actualization. Their studies showed that TM increases the extent to which a person moves toward the mature end of Maslow's[6] need hierarchy, or toward a position where he seeks to be mature on the job, to exercise a high degree of autonomy and independence, to adopt a long-time perspective, to become flexible in adapting to circumstances, to move toward self-controlled and highly motivated, and to develop increasing and specialized skills. Seeman, Nidich, and Banta[7] also studied the relationship between TM and self-actualization and found support for the Ferguson and Gowan study. Using Shostrom's[8] personal-orientation inventory they were able to monitor changes in the direction of self-actualization for TM practitioners.

So the stage was set for a research study which would deal specifically with the impact of TM at work. The early research gave every indication that TM had some very positive benefits, not only from the pure physiological perspective, but also from the position of TM and work-group behavior. Indications were that TM improved dexterity, problem-solving capability, work quality, reaction time and self-actualization. This broad range of variables included not only the kinds of things which would enhance job performance for hourly or production workers, but offered great hope for managerial levels as well. The self-actualization studies, in particular, indicated great potential for upper-level employees and TM.)

But many members of both the scientific and the business communities remained very skeptical. They were concerned about the pseudo-ideological aspects which they read into the practice of TM. Meditators might have the potential to become better and more productive workers, but would they? Might they not waste their new-found productivity potential on nonproductive activities?

These were the issues which formed the foundation for the studies of TM and productivity which follow.

TM and Productivity

A systematic view of the effects of Transcendental Meditation and productivity required a large and sophisticated study which would investigate many different aspects of TM and approach the question of productivity from several different perspectives. The work that will be presented here actually consisted of two different studies. The first was an analysis of the impact of TM upon the employee. Here the approach was to measure changes in work-oriented variables, such as productivity or turnover for meditators as a result of TM experience. (The results of this study were first presented at Michigan State University in 1973 during the American Institute of Decision Sciences Symposium.[9] The study, itself, was published in the "Proceeding" of that meeting, and then appeared in a more sophisticated form in a 1974 *Academy of Management Journal* article entitled "TM and Productivity."[10] The second part of the overall work was a meditators versus nonmeditators study which focused upon the essential differences between the two groups, again in terms of several different productivity variables. Taken together, I feel that the two studies systematically provide thorough scientific evidence for the powerful impact of TM upon productivity. But to learn about how TM has an impact upon the organization and its participants in terms of the management language that we have become accustomed to using, the two studies will be presented individually.

Subjects

The first study, and to the best of my knowledge the
pioneering study of TM and productivity at work, was a study
of the effects of TM upon meditators. Subjects for the study
were located by going to several TM teaching centers within
New York, Pennsylvania, and Ohio, and obtaining mailing
lists for persons who had been trained in the method of TM.
Working with grant funds provided by the Gannon College
Faculty Senate, persons on the lists were randomly selected and
contacted via the telephone. Three preliminary questions were
asked in an effort to sort the original population into a useful
group of admissible study subjects:

1. Are you actively meditating?
2. Do you have a full-time job?
3. Is it the same job that you had before you started to
meditate?

Only persons who provided positive answers to these three
questions were invited to participate in the study. Thus the
presurvey interview eliminated persons who had been trained
in TM, but who had, for one reason or another, given up the
practice. Also, persons with part-time jobs such as students or
housewives were eliminated from the study. And since the
strategy was to determine the impact of TM upon job performance it was determined at the onset that persons who had
changed jobs since learning TM should be eliminated also. We
wanted to include only those persons who were working at
jobs which they held both before and after TM.

The final sample included one hundred meditators whose
average age was twenty-seven years, and average length of TM
experience was thirteen months. There were sixty-eight men
and thirty women within the group, and 76 percent were
married.

The Study

A questionnaire was designed to obtain information about
the subjects. In addition to questions about age, marital status,

and meditating experience, information was sought about the organizational environment of the subject and about changes in productivity variables as a result of meditation.

In terms of the organizational environment, participants were asked to supply information about four different aspects.

1. Size
2. Task complexity
3. Organization structure
4. Job level

Although the first two, size and task complexity, did not prove to be of interest in terms of the analysis of data, the second two provided a great deal of interest and impact upon the final results. Subjects were asked to provide information about the kind of structure where they worked ("1," or autocratic, versus "5," or democratic), and the level of their own jobs within that structure.

The questionnaire also asked questions regarding six measures of productivity.

1. Job satisfaction
2. Performance
3. Turnover potential
4. Relationship with supervisor
5. Relationships with others
6. Motivation to climb

Exhibit 6.1 is a sample of the survey instrument.

Exhibit 6.1

QUESTIONNAIRE A

A STUDY OF THE EFFECTS OF
TRANSCENDENTAL MEDITATION AT WORK

GANNON
COLLEGE   GRADUATE SCHOOL   ERIE, PA.
                        OF
              BUSINESS ADMINISTRATION

You have been selected to participate in this study because of the fact that you have become involved in Transcendental Meditation. The purpose of this questionnaire is to gather information about the effects of TM upon your working life. Please answer the following questions as accurately and sincerely as possible. You may be assured that your particular answers will be held confidential and that your personal identity will be lost in the statistical analysis which is to follow.

Thank you,
Dr. David R. Frew

A. Following is a list of questions about yourself and your meditating experience. Please fill in the appropriate blanks.

1. How long have you been meditating? _____

2. Do you consider yourself to be an active meditator? _____

3. Age _____ 4. Sex _____ 5. Marital Status _____

B. The questions in this section relate to the kind of organization that you work in. Please check the appropriate blanks.

1. Approximately how many people are employed at the location or plant where you work? _____

2. Please identify the general kind of work that your company or plant is doing:

    a. Rapidly changing and complex _____
    b. Relatively complicated _____
    c. Fairly stable _____
    d. Routine and repetitive _____

3. Please typify the kind of structure and/or managerial atmosphere which best describes your organization:

    a. Relatively rigid military-type atmosphere _____
    b. Although military or bureaucratic by design the people and procedures decrease the formality _____
    c. Relatively informal with few levels of management _____
    d. Very democratic - no apparent differences in levels between participants _____

4. At which level of the organization do you work?

    a. Upper management _____
    b. Middle management _____

    c.   First level supervision or clerical _____

    d.   Production level _____

C.   The questions below are designed to determine the changes (if any) which have come about in your attitudes toward and performance on your job as a result of transcendental meditation. Please check the appropriate blank:

I. QUESTIONS REGARDING THE JOB ITSELF

1.   Since meditating, I have found that the work that I do is

    a.   Much more exciting and challenging _____
    b.   More pleasant and acceptable _____
    c.   Unchanged _____
    d.   Less interesting than before _____
    e.   Completely boring, almost impossible _____

2.   In terms of the demands or objectives of the organization my performance since TM

    a.   Has improved greatly _____
    b.   Is slightly improved _____
    c.   Has remained the same _____
    d.   Is slightly worse than before _____
    e.   Has fallen quite drastically _____

3.   Which of the following is your criteria for answering the above question?

    a.   Incentive standards _____
    b.   Measured daywork _____
    c.   Feedback from your boss _____
    d.   Feedback from fellow workers _____
    e.   Your personal observation _____

4.   Since becoming involved in TM my intentions of looking for another job might best be described as

    a.   More than ever before I am thinking about
        a change of jobs   _____
    b.   I am considering a job change   _____
    c.   There is no change   _____
    d.   I am beginning to feel less like
        changing jobs   _____
    e.   I have become convinced that I
        should stay where I am   _____

II. QUESTIONS REGARDING RELATIONSHIPS AT WORK

5.   Since meditating my relationship with my supervisor

    a.   Has improved tremendously   _____
    b.   Is slightly improved   _____
    c.   Has not changed   _____
    d.   Has worsened slightly   _____
    e.   Is much worse   _____

6.   Relationships with the people that I work with have

    a.   Improved tremendously   _____
    b.   Become slightly better   _____
    c.   Remained unchanged   _____
    d.   Deteriorated slightly   _____
    e.   Become much worse   _____

7.   All things considered (the company as well as the people in it) my ambitions or aspirations have changed in the following way since meditating

    a.   I am increasing my efforts to move up the
        organizational ladder at any cost   _____
    b.   I am slightly more ambitious   _____
    c.   There has been no change   _____
    d.   I am generally more content with
        my present position.   _____
    e.   I am not interested in a promotion _____

Control Groups

In an effort to provide statistical control for the experiment, two separate control groups were designed. These groups were devised to provide answers to two fundamental sets of questions:

(1) What if TM subjects thought that their productivity variables had changed in a positive direction since TM, but their bosses or coworkers viewed them in a different or opposite manner? In short, could TM simply give a person the illusion of his own increasing productivity?

(2) Could it be that TM simply provides an initial lift which is no different than any other training or learning

experience? Perhaps a person could take a speed-reading course or go to a seminar or join the Toastmasters or get involved in any other kind of activity to achieve the same basic effect. My major concern was to design a study which would guard against these two problems while gathering information about the effect of TM upon productivity.

The first control measure included a separate questionnaire. This instrument was exactly the same as the previous research instrument (Exhibit 6.1) except that it was reworded so that it could be answered by coworkers or supervisors of the survey subjects. An overall group of 50 persons who were either supervisors or coworkers of the TM subjects agreed to rate the TM group in terms of the same items that the subjects responded to. The control group was not asked to answer questions about the organizational environment.

The meditator, for example, was asked:

Since meditating, relationships with the people you work with have . . . . ,

Then the person's coworker in the control group was asked:

Since meditating, his relationships with his coworkers have . . . .

A sample of this questionnaire is included in exhibit 6.2.

Exhibit 6.2

QUESTIONNAIRE B

A STUDY OF THE EFFECTS OF
TRANSCENDENTAL MEDITATION AT WORK

GANNON
COLLEGE   GRADUATE SCHOOL   ERIE, PA.
                         OF
               BUSINESS ADMINISTRATION

You have been selected to participate in this study because of the fact that a coworker (or subordinate) has begun the practice of Transcendental

Meditation. We would appreciate your answering the following questions about the changes in your colleague's work patterns since meditating. You may be assured that your answers will be held in the strictest of confidence.

Thank you,
David R. Frew

A.   In your working relationship with the subject are you

  1.   A coworker or equal? _____

  2.   A superordinate (supervisor)? _____

  3.   Other (please specify)? _____

B.   The questions below are designed to determine the changes (if any) which have come about in the subject's attitude toward and performance on the job since practicing TM. Please check the appropriate blank.

  1.   Since meditating he seems to find his work

      a.   Much more exciting and challenging _____
      b.   More pleasant and acceptable _____
      c.   Unchanged _____
      d.   Less interesting than before _____
      e.   Completely boring, almost impossible _____

  2.   His performance since beginning TM

      a.   Has improved greatly _____
      b.   Is slightly improved _____
      c.   Has remained the same _____
      d.   Is slightly worse than before _____
      e.   Has fallen quite drastically _____

  3.   Since meditating, his intentions of looking for a different job seem to have

      a.   Increased greatly _____
      b.   Increased moderately _____
      c.   Remained the same _____
      d.   Decreased slightly _____
      e.   Decreased greatly _____

  4.   Since meditating, his relationship with his supervisor

      a.   Has improved tremendously _____

b. Is slightly improved _____
c. Has not changed _____
d. Has worsened slightly _____
e. Is much worse _____

5. Relationships with his coworkers have

a. Improved tremendously _____
b. Become slightly better _____
c. Remained unchanged _____
d. Deteriorated slightly _____
e. Become much worse _____

6. His aspirations or ambitions appear to have

a. Increased greatly _____
b. Increased slightly _____
c. Remained the same _____
d. Decreased slightly _____
e. Decreased greatly _____

7. Which of the following is your criteria for answering Question #2?

a. Incentive standards _____
b. Measured daywork _____
c. Feedback from your boss _____
d. Feedback from fellow workers _____
e. Your personal observation _____

The second control group consisted of graduate students who were asked to refer to any kind of program or phenomenon which had taken place within the immediate past and to report changes within their productivity which resulted from this experience. Particular kinds of experiences reported by this control group varied, ranging from graduate courses to management seminars and religious experiences. But each participant in the final control group was able to isolate some recent experience and then to try and relate the effect of that experience to his particular work situation.

This second control group used the same research instrument that was used by the first group, but filled it out in terms of their own non-TM experiences.

The Results of the Study

Data from the TM practitioners, the coworkers and the

non-TM control group were collected and placed in tabular form for analysis. But before pursuing these results and their implications, the measuring system should be explained.

Measuring Productivity

All of the productivity questions on the research instruments used herein were designed to measure the extent and direction of change since a person had begun to practice TM. To learn about a person's feeling of job satisfaction, for example, he was asked to complete the following item:

Since meditating I find that the work that I do is

 a. Much more exciting and challenging
 b. More pleasant and acceptable
 c. Unchanged
 d. Less interesting than before
 e. Completely boring, almost impossible

The participant was to select (for this and each other item in the questionnaire) the most appropriate answer.

To convert to a quantitative measure of change the answers were translated into numbers. Thus a five-point scale resulted which ranged from an answer of "a" (1.0) or a strong positive change, through "c" (3.0) or no change, to "e" (5.0) which indicated a strong negative change.

In terms of the quantitative measures which appear in the tables and graphs which are to follow, values from 2.9 to 1.0 indicate a positive or increasing value, while values from 3.1 to 5.0 suggest a negative or decreasing value. If a group of subjects had answered the job satisfaction question with an average of 2.0 it would suggest increasing job satisfaction. An answer of 4.0 would suggest decreasing job satisfaction. Table 6.1 contains a summary of each research variable and its measuring system.

If TM was to be a positive influence upon productivity variables, meditators had to answer the item as follows:

The Data

Actual results, including the three different groups (meditator, non-TM control group, and coworkers) are assembled in Table 6.2.

Table 6.1
A Summary of the Measuring System

Variable	Change				
	1.0	1.1 → 2.9	3.0	3.1 → 4.9	5.0
Job Satisfaction	Max Positive	Increasing	No	Decreasing	Max Negative
Performance	Max Positive	Improving	No	Degenerating	Max Negative
Turnover Propensity	Max Positive	Increasing	No	Decreasing	Max Negative
Relationship W/Boss	Max Positive	Better	No	Worse	Max Negative
Relationships W/Others	Max Positive	Better	No	Worse	Max Negative
Climb Orientation	Max Positive	Increasing	No	Decreasing	Max Negative

Increasing Job Satisfaction	(2.9 - 1.0)
Better Performance	(2.9 - 1.0)
Lower Turnover Propensity	(3.1 - 5.0)
Better Relationships with Supervisor	(2.9 - 1.0)
Better Relationships with Coworkers	(2.9 - 1.0)

The meditating group reported that TM led to positive increases in job satisfaction and performance. A reduced turnover propensity, improved relationships with both supervisors and coworkers, and a lower motivation to climb the organizational ladder. The magnitude of these changes is shown in Figure 6.1.

Table 6.2
The Effect of T.M. upon Productivity

Variable	Meditators		Control Group		Coworkers	
	Av.	Sig. of Diff. from 3.0	Av.	Sig. of Diff. from Subjts.	Av.	Sig. of Diff. from Subjts.
y_1	2.1	.01	2.9	.01	2.5	.05
y_2	1.9	.01	3.2	.01	2.1	NO
y_3	3.4	.05	2.8	.05	3.0	NO
y_4	2.0	.01	2.5	.05	1.5	.05
y_5	1.6	.01	2.7	.01	1.6	NO
y_6	3.6	.01	2.7	.01	2.3	.01

y_1 - signifies Job Satisfaction

y_2 - signfies Performance

y_3 - signifies Turnover Propensity

y_4 - signifies Relations w/Supervisor

y_5 - signifies Relations w/Coworkers

y_6 - signifies Climb Orientation

Comparative data for the control and the coworkers is included in Table 6.2. The control group answered that their particular non-TM experiences:

1. Increased job satisfaction (but not by as much as TM)
2. Decreased performance
3. Increased turnover propensity
4. Benefited relationships (but not as much as TM)
5. Increased climb orientation

It might be concluded from this data that with the exception of the sixth variable, climb orientation, the meditating group appears to have achieved substantial gains in productivity. This finding is supported by the results of the control group which are either smaller in magnitude, or moving in the opposite direction in each case. Thus TM appears to cause changes in productivity which are different from the changes which might be caused by other kinds of phenomena such as management seminars, training programs, or college courses.

Data for coworkers, which is also included in Table 6.2 will be analyzed more fully within the next section of this chapter.

Figure 6.1
Charges in Productivity after TM

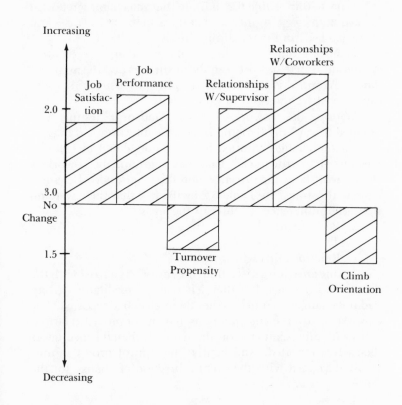

Statistical Analysis

To insure that the changes observed within the meditating group were not caused by chance or random variation, statistical tests were performed upon each of the three sets of data (meditators, control, and coworkers).

First, each of the averages provided by the meditating group was tested for the significance of the difference between the particular average and the scalar midvalue of 3.0 which indicated no change. For example, meditators reported that their job satisfaction increased to 2.1 from the midpoint, or 3.0. The statistical question asked, then, was this: Is 2.1 significantly different from 3.0?

Data within Table 6.2 indicate that the changes reported by meditators were significant[11] at the .01 level in five cases and at the 0.5 level in the remaining instance.

Control-group statistics indicate that there were significant differences between the meditators and the nonmeditators. Again, this lends support to the proposition that TM caused positive increases in productivity.

Within the coworker group, statistical testing was oriented toward the hypothesis that the direction and magnitude of the change reported by meditators could be collaborated by their coworkers. Taken as a group, the coworkers agreed with both the direction and the magnitude of change. This is illustrated in Table 6.2 by the fact that there were no significant differences in three of the areas:

a. Performance
b. Turnover propensity
c. Relationships with coworkers

In one area, job satisfaction, the coworkers agreed with the direction of change, but they felt that the meditating group had not changed as much as they themselves had reported. The coworkers saw the meditators as having improved relationships with others, much more dramatically than the meditators themselves reported. And finally, the control group significantly disagreed with the overall direction of change for the sixth variable, climb orientation. They viewed the meditators as more highly motivated to climb than they had been before meditation.

Meditators as Viewed by Their Coworkers

The data which was provided by the supervisors and fellow-workers of the meditating group helps to provide an interesting and useful insight into the way that meditators are viewed by the people around them at work.

First, it is important to note that meditators were objectively seen to be changed individuals at work. Practical experience would suggest that this in itself is indicative of some rather dramatic behavioral changes by the meditators themselves. Coworkers corroborated the change in three of the dimensions studied herein. They agree that the meditator's performance or work output is greater, that he is less inclined to leave for another company, and that the quality of his interpersonal relationships had increased. The results are illustrated in Figure 6.2.

There was some disagreement, however, on the other variables. Coworkers felt that the meditator's job satisfaction had increased but did not think that his satisfaction had increased as dramatically as the meditators themselves suggested that it had.

It is also interesting to note that the coworkers felt that the meditators had made far greater improvements in their relationships with their bosses than the meditators reported.

Finally the coworker group disagreed with meditators' views of their ambition to climb. While the meditators, themselves, reported a significant decrease in motivation, they were viewed as having more climb orientation. Perhaps this finding is linked to the previous result in that the boss and particularly the "boss-employee relationship" is crucial to advancement in most organizations.

In summary, then, meditators are viewed by their fellow workers as more productive in terms of each of the dimensions included here. It would have been very interesting to interview these people about their feelings toward the meditators that they worked with. Were they threatened by these sudden increases in productive behavior? Could the increases in performance and other productivity criteria have caused the meditators any unique difficulties at work? The data suggest that if there were any interpersonal problems, the meditators were able to cope with them in an effective way.

Figure 6.2
Meditators as Viewed by
Their Coworkers

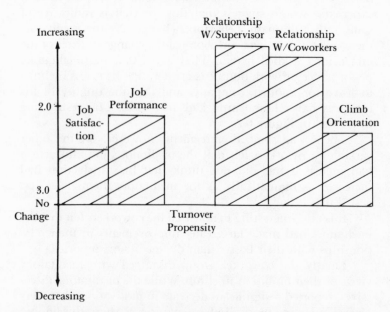

Now that we have overviewed the general results of the study, the next step will be to look at each of the six dimensions of productivity on an individual basis. Analyses of job satisfaction, output, turnover, relationships with coworkers, relationships with the supervisor, and motivation to climb, are included in the following sections of this chapter.

Job Satisfaction

Perhaps the most talked about and written about variable in the literature of organizational behavior is job satisfaction. Theorists have been interested in this aspect of job performance since the turn of the century. And while the orientations have changed from year to year and from study to study, one trend has prevailed over the many investigations of job satisfaction. That is confusion!

Perhaps no other single line of investigation has universally turned up so many different answers to the same question: "What is it that makes people particularly happy or excited about their jobs?"

Fredrick Hertzberg[12] was one of the first theorists to recognize the incredible complexity and the depth of individual perceptions of jobs in his dual-factor theory. This work suggested that there were two different kinds of job satisfiers: those which make us feel particularly good about our jobs, and those which cause us to feel particularly negative about them. In other words, it was possible to be both satisfied and dissatisfied with our jobs. While a great deal of controversy still rages over Hertzberg's experiments, he has done a great deal to systemize and collect previous studies.

Porter and Lawler[13] later showed the impact of intrinsic factors upon job satisfaction. Their work has highlighted the possibility that traditional job satisfaction factors, such as wages or fringe benefits, do not meet the complex internal needs of persons who work.

Much of the later literature has floundered about the supercomplex issues of differences of people, the dynamics of relationships, psychological development or maturity, and economics, while trying to arrive at a sensible strategy for increasing the job satisfaction of people at work.

The study, herein, suggests a much simpler approach. The strategy is akin to magic inasmuch as it does not make a great deal of immediate logical sense from the perspective of the job satisfaction literature. But the simple fact remains that meditators find that job satisfaction increases as a result of their meditation.

The management strategy which is suggested is very straightforward:

To increase job satisfaction, one needs to reduce the level of stress at work.

TM or any other stress-reducing technique can be applied in situations where managers or others seek to improve job satisfaction.

But does TM actually improve a job or a job situation? No, probably not, but it would appear that TM actually helps the person in the job to more adequately cope with his situation. Since we define ourselves in terms of what we do, it is very possible to allow ourselves to degenerate into increasingly bad job-role self-concept positions. "Our job is not quite going right," thus we blame ourselves, which makes the job seem even worse. We may react to this by blaming ourselves even more. The end result is an inseparable hodgepodge of negative feedback.

Perhaps what TM does is to help the person to sort through the various impacts of the job versus the self; to see that a person in a less than perfect situation is not necessarily a bad person. Thus, the relative calm and tranquility which TM brings may give a person a whole new perspective on his job.

And perhaps it is also true that as a person becomes more able to view his job in an objective sense, he is in a more powerful position to effect changes at work. So, in an indirect way, TM might even affect the job itself.

Output

Perhaps the most fundamentally important variable within a study of productivity is output itself. Output is probably linked more clearly to the ultimate success or failure of a company than any of the other individual variables studied here. If output increases, particularly for production level employees, it would be difficult to imagine how the overall position (in terms of profit or other criterion) of a company could not logically improve.

Meditators universally reported that TM increased their job performance in simple output terms. Depending upon the kind of job, the criterion used for reporting this change in performance varied. Production-level employees, for example, reported that their average weekly earnings on Industrial Engineering Standards had increased. Managers and other nonproduction workers reported other kinds of criterion such as reduced scheduling difficulty, comparison with past performance, or just a simple "feeling of efficiency." But the universal response was one of increased productivity.

This result is not all that surprising in light of the psychophysiology of stress. Highly stressed persons are not only less adept at mental work, but have higher reaction time and reduced dexterity. It was to be expected, barring organizational or psychological complications, that as TM reduced aggregate stress, productivity would increase.

Some of the testimonial data from meditators was even more amazing than the results of the statistical data. Several executives who said that they were working from ten to twenty hours overtime a week just to keep up with the demands of their jobs, stated that they were now able to approach their jobs in a more efficient manner, so that they could easily do sixty hours work in forty. One salesman who was interviewed reported that he had increased his sales by more than 50 percent as a result of TM.

The data, the testimonials, and the physiological literature, taken together, suggest a very powerful relationship between TM and output. This result was valid for productivity, in general, meaning that TM was a useful tool for both management-level employees and production-level employees.

Turnover

There are a number of ways to study turnover. And like the job-satisfaction issue, turnover has traditionally been a popular variable within the scientific community. "What causes employees to leave their jobs" is not only an interesting theoretical problem, but an extremely important practical issue. Many millions of dollars are spent each year to replace and retrain employees who change their jobs.

While academicians have struggled with the theoretical aspects of this problem, many companies have developed programs to try to help themselves with their turnover problems. Some have begun to utilize the exit interview to try to gather after-the-fact data about why employees leave their jobs.

The study herein took a rather unique, but powerful approach to the study of turnover. Instead of viewing turnover statistics or data from exit interviews, we felt that the best approach was simply to ask the employees themselves if they were looking for another job. The variable which results is called *turnover propensity* and measures the extent to which employees are interested in changing companies.

Consider for example the radically different positions of two different kinds of companies. Company A had only one percent turnover last year. For some reason, its employees are very happy with their jobs and don't think that they could improve their positions via a job change. Company B also had a 1 percent turnover rate, but this was because the employees were simply not able to leave for another job due to the bad economic situation that year. The ramifications of the differences between these two companies are very broad and very important in terms of management practice. But if a company were to base its information primarily upon exit interviews or through turnover statistics, then it might be looking at its employees through rose-colored glasses.

The "turnover propensity" variable is a much better approach in this regard. It illustrates "potential" turnover problems and thus provides more useful information for either theoretical or practical use.

The results of the study suggested that TM reduces the tendency of employees to want to change companies. This is surely related to the job satisfaction issue which was discussed previously. Reduced stress levels allow persons to see their jobs much more clearly and to sort out the job characteristics which are generic to the job itself or related to other job-related items, such as the personalities of individuals at work, or specific characteristics of the economic environment, such as inflation.

So, while the theoretical controversies rage on, it is reassuring to note that direct improvements in the job satisfaction/turnover picture of a company can be implemented through the application of stress-reducing techniques such as TM.

Interpersonal Relationships

The area where TM appeared to have the greatest impact, in terms of magnitude, was in relationships with both supervisors and coworkers. The meditators reported improvements which averaged 1.2 scale points in their relationships with supervisors and coworkers. Since the average change for the other four variables was .8 scale points, it might be concluded that stress reduction has its greatest impact upon interpersonal relationships. As aggregate stress is reduced, persons are much more capable of dealing effectively with a variety of people including their bosses.

These relationships also appear to acquire an improved quality from the perspective of the coworkers themselves. The control data strongly suggested that coworkers viewed the meditators as having improved their interpersonal skills.

Evidently the reduced stress levels of meditators lead to reduction of organizational conflict. Communications become more clear, problems of noise and interference diminish, and both meditators and their coworkers realize the cumulative benefits of increased productivity.

Motivation to Climb

Some of the most interesting and, at the same time, perplexing results of this research surrounded the motivation-to-climb variable. Originally we had hoped to see how the reduction of stress affected a person's ambition to climb the

organizational "ladder." We had viewed this as a tandem
variable with turnover propensity.

It was also proposed at the beginning of the study that an
increase in productivity would be signaled by an increased
motivation to climb. The results of the study, however, were
contradictory. Meditators reported that they had less (.6 scale
points) motivation to climb the organization since beginning
TM.

At first we wondered if this might not be connected to the
job-satisfaction issue. As job satisfaction increases, a person
becomes more content with his particular activity at work and,
consequently, less concerned about a promotion to the next
level. But a more perplexing problem emerged when we
viewed the data from the coworkers group. The coworkers of
the meditating group perceived the meditators' motivation to
climb as having increased by .7 scale points rather than having
decreased.

Thus the following explanation for the motivation to
climb variable emerged after some discussion with a number of
the subjects.

Almost all of us have either observed or been personally
involved in a situation where an employee is concerned about
promotion at any cost. Many volumes have been written about
the back-stabbing and politicking which is said to exist in
most major corporations. Whether these are exaggerated
accounts of reality or not it is entirely obvious that our work
culture is very promotion- and success-oriented. To be promoted is good. To work at one level for a very long time is
suggestive of failure. Thus, the pressures exist to work and
strive for a promotion. Many people seem to get so caught up
in this promotion syndrome that they devote more of their
productive effort to political maneuvering than they do to their
jobs. In the long run, this kind of behavior and its associated
stress may be counterproductive to the possibility of promotion as well as the job itself.

TM may work to reduce the stress and anxiety about
promotion thus redirecting productive energy toward the

accomplishment of the task itself. The ultimate effect of this phenomenon, as viewed from the eyes of coworkers may be such an energetic increase in productive behavior at work that the meditator is viewed as significantly more ambitious.

Perhaps, then, the effect of TM upon the motivation of a worker is both negative and good. As stress is reduced, the worker becomes more concerned with good performance on a day-to-day basis and less concerned about a promotion to the next higher level. As a result of this increased efficiency, his chances for a promotion may increase more substantially than they would if he were to direct his attention toward "success" rather than productivity itself.

The Executive Versus the
Production Worker

One of our most fundamental questions at the design stage of the TM study surrounded the effects of TM upon various kinds of employees. Would TM or other stress-relieving devices have the same impact upon the managers and executives of a company that it would have upon the production-level personnel? In other words, did organizational level have an effect upon the relative impacts of stress reduction and productivity which would follow the application of TM?

To test this question the data was sorted into two groups according to answers furnished by the meditating group. The "Low" group consisted of persons who worked at production or clerical jobs. The "High" group was composed of persons who worked at executive or managerial levels within their organizations. The data was then re-evaluated to see if there were differences between the High and Low groups.

The results, which are tabulated in Table 6.3, suggest some very real differences between the executive and the production worker. For five out of six productivity variables, upper-level employees enjoyed significantly greater gains (either at the .01 or the .05 level) in productivity as a result of TM.[14]

Table 6.3
The Effect of Organizational Level
upon Productivity Variables

Variable	Ave.	Organizational Level		
		Low	High	Significance Level
Y_1	2.1	2.5	1.9	.01
Y_2	1.9	2.3	1.6	.01
Y_3	3.4	2.5	4.0	.05
Y_4	2.0	2.3	1.8	.05
Y_5	1.6	2.0	1.3	.01
Y_6	3.6	3.5	3.6	none

Y_1 - signifies Job Satisfaction

Y_2 - signifies Performance

Y_3 - signfies Turnover Propensity

Y_4 - signifies Relations w/Supervisor

Y_5 - signifies Relations w/Coworkers

Y_6 - signifies Climb Orientation

Using *job satisfaction* as an example, all meditators reported a change from 3.0 (the scalar midpoint) to 2.1 or .9 scale points as a result of TM. This clearly suggests that their job satisfaction increased. But in breaking the data down into two groups, the High group which was composed of executives, managers, and engineers, reported an improvement of 1.1 scale points (1.9), while production-level employees, the Low group, reported an improvement of only .5 scale points.

It might be concluded, therefore, that while TM is a useful strategy to employ throughout an organization, the benefits are most powerful among upper-level employees.

This makes good sense in light of the previous chapters which dealt with management theory. If we can take TM (the technique) to be a constant value stress-relieving tool, then it follows in logic that it would alleviate the most stress within the highest stress situations. And, as we saw earlier within this book, there is a great deal of pressure from both the perspectives of task efficiency and structural design in the top levels of organizations. So the lower-level employees are, to a large extent, shielded from many of the stresses which are absorbed by the managers who are trying to deal with complex tasks from within their outdated autocratic structures.

TM and Organizational Structure

Another question which logically follows is this: How does the structure of an organization affect the impact of TM? Is the technique any more useful in a democratic rather than an autocratic setting?

To test this question the data was again sorted into two groups. But this time the meditators' responses to an organizational structure question were used to divide the data into autocratic versus democratic groups. The data for each of the six dimensions of productivity were re-evaluated and placed in Table 6.4.

It was determined from statistical analysis that three of the six variables reflected significant increases in productivity between the two groups.[14] The three particular variables which were affected by both TM and organizational structure were the interpersonal relationship variables (both boss and coworker dimensions) and the productivity variable.

It can be concluded, then, that while TM provides overall benefits in productivity, these increases in productivity are most dramatic within democratic organizations.

Again, the structural analysis makes sense in light of what we know about organizational behavior. In the previous section of this chapter it was found that upper-level employees

Table 6.4
The Effect of Organizational Structure
upon Productivity Variables

Variable	Ave.	Structure		
		Autoc.	Democ.	Significance Level
Y_1	2.1	2.1	2.0	none
Y_2	1.9	2.0	1.7	.01
Y_3	3.4	2.7	2.5	none
Y_4	2.0	2.3	1.5	.01
Y_5	1.6	1.9	1.2	.01
Y_6	3.6	3.8	3.5	none

Y_1 - signifies Job Satisfaction

Y_2 - signifies Performance

Y_3 - signifies Turnover Propensity

Y_4 - signifies Relations w/Supervisor

Y_5 - signifies Relations w/Coworkers

Y_6 - signifies Climb Orientation

benefit most from TM because they bear the brunt of many stresses which impact their organizations. Evidently, what happens as organizational structures evolve from autocratic to more democratic forms, is that the stresses become more commonly distributed among the employees. This increase in stress would be particularly evident within the interpersonal relationship variables. High levels of stress would naturally lead to a great variety of problems in terms of people's relationships with each other. But, at the same time, good democratic process requires a solid foundation of interpersonal relationships. In other words, an autocratic organization may run fairly well on the basis of efficient rules and regulations either with or without much attention being paid to the interpersonal aspects of the organization. Since democratic management presupposes the continued existence of quality interaction, the interpersonal aspects of a participative organization are critically important.

The results, therefore, are suggesting that relationships with the boss and coworkers are benefited much more powerfully within democratic (1.5 and 1.8 scale points respectively) organizations than they are on the average (1.0 and 1.4 scale points). The results also suggest a corresponding advantage within the output variable. This would appear to be very logical since output is strongly linked to interpersonal relationship quality within democratic organizations.

The Study in Retrospect

After assembling and reviewing the completed data from this first study it became clear to me that I had struck upon a powerful tool for the improvement of productivity. My own study of organization had convinced me years prior to any knowledge of TM that work stress was a major factor underlying many if not all of the primary problems of organizations. Perhaps, in retrospect, my first several professional years in the field of Organizational Behavior had consisted of a series of sincere but misdirected and inefficient theoretical attempts toward an answer to the dilemma of "highly stressed workers working in a superstressful environment."

So after all of the hours and days of attempting to diagnose and treat organizational difficulties via theoretically oriented techniques, a simple thing like TM comes along and provides powerful cures for these complex behavior and structural problems. The implications are quite clear: no matter how we choose to look at behavior in organizations, it would seem that we always end up at the root or component part of the organization, the individual. So perhaps the treatment of organizational sickness must begin with the participant rather than the structure or the process. Perhaps an organization which is staffed with competent and productive persons cannot help but be a great success.

To be quite honest, my empirical study of TM and productivity began from the posture of skepticism. My first conceptual connections between TM and work led me to believe that meditators might find work to be distasteful. Consequently, my original expectation was that TM would reduce rather than increase at least some dimensions of productivity. It was the results of the study which caused me to drop my other theoretical interests and pursue a better scientific understanding of TM in the literatures of physiology and psychology, not the opposite. It is this particular sequence of events (which is probably unique from my own experience since many such experiments are designed to gather data in support of an existing theory) which had led to the overwhelming enthusiasm which I have developed for TM as a productivity tool.

At this point, my feeling is that Transcendental Meditation may be the single most powerful tool for dealing with the problems of organizational life. The theoretical work and the empirical work both indicate the viability of a stress-reducing tool for dealing with problems at work. The TM literature, both theoretical and empirical, supports the supposition that transcendental meditation is a powerful stress reducer.

Meditators report that TM leads to significant changes in their approach to their jobs. They are happier at work, more productive and get along much better with the people around them. And taken in its simplest form, how could anyone who is interested in improving their job or the jobs of the people around them not get excited about such a result? But there are still some skeptics among us, and for the sake of those who refuse to be influenced by a single study or a set of statistical tests, this first research project was just not enough!

The Need for Another Study

Somehow, the TM and productivity articles which emerged during the first year that I spent in this area of study received an overwhelming amount of recognition. Almost overnight I was being deluged with invitations to present my research to various scholarly or business groups. After a few dozen such engagements, a very subtle reality began to creep into my awareness: "Not everyone believed me!" My reaction to this was complex. At first I was upset and defensive. "Look, how can you deny this evidence?" I would say. "I don't need a rationalization." "You need more proof," the audience skeptic would retort.

So after cataloguing the various critical analyses of my study, my next and most sensible step was to begin the design of a second study—one which would provide answers to the criticisms of the first.

Three basic concerns seemed to repeat themselves as I presented my research design and my results.

1. The size of the study
2. The lack of a meditators-nonmeditators design
3. The validity of the instrument (questionnaire)

So I began the design of "TM and Productivity II" with the major goal of alleviating these problem areas.

The Sample Size

Even though the statistical techniques employed during the first study allowed for the relatively small sample sizes, and the data still provided significant differences, a few of the more practically oriented individuals who listened to my research presentations objected to the "small," as they viewed it, sample. They wondered if a larger experiment which was drawn from a greater geographic area might not change the nature of the results.

The design of Study II would, then, have to include more subjects and would have to draw these subjects from a broader geographic area than the three states which were represented by the first study.

The Meditators Versus
Nonmeditators Design

A number of persons who read the first study were also concerned about the fact that the original design was not a meditator versus nonmeditator approach. Study I simply asked about changes over time. Did meditators experience improvements in their working lives? And while the control group provided some of the answers to this design challenge, the first study was not specifically oriented toward uncovering the differences between meditators and nonmeditators at work. In fact, it was suggested by some that the control measures provided by the first study were not sufficient to insure against the possibility that any random group of workers might report that their productivity was just as high as that of the meditating group.

So the approach of the second study was to be meditators versus nonmeditators in design. A single instrument was to be designed and distributed to an equal number of meditating and nonmeditating workers. The data analysis would then focus upon the differences between these two groups.

The Instrument Design

A few of the persons who read my research were concerned about the instrument which was used to gather the data. They suggested that an instrument such as this one which was specifically designed to carry out a single research project, might not be entirely valid. In other words, it might not measure exactly what it purported to measure. From my own perspective this particular criticism appeared to be both the most serious and the most useful. Thus this instrument-design question required some kind of special attention during the second study.

A number of different alternatives presented themselves, but the best single approach seemed to be the design of a completely new instrument. The logic underlying this alternative was that if a completely different instrument (questionnaire) could be applied to the same problem (Does TM increase productivity?) and gain the same results, then we would have answered many of the questions regarding the validity of our results.

TM and Productivity II

Thus the second study was motivated by the desire to learn more about the impact of TM upon productivity, and also by the desire to answer the critical analyses of the first study.

The Instrument

Perhaps the most important aspect of Study II was to be a redesigned research instrument. A great deal of work at the beginning of the project was oriented toward the design of a new questionnaire to elicit data from both the subjects and the nonmeditators. The revised instrument which is shown in Exhibit 6.3 is more compact than the previous questionnaire. But it contains all of the data which comprised the one from the first study.

Exhibit 6.3

JOB SATISFACTION

A PERSONAL INVENTORY

by

DR. DAVID R. FREW
GRADUATE SCHOOL OF BUSINESS
GANNON COLLEGE

The purpose of this questionnaire is to help supply information about jobs and the things which make jobs particularly meaningful or pleasant. Please work quickly, and answer as many of the items as you can. If you have any additional comments, they can be added to the back of the sheet. You may be assured that

your particular answers will be held in the strictest confidence and that your
personal identity will be lost in the statistical analysis which is to follow.

Please respond to each statement below by circling the appropriate initials:

SA = Strongly Agree	MD = Moderately Disagree
A = Agree	D = Disagree
MA = Moderately Agree	SD = Strongly Disagree

1. In general, my job is very positive aspect of my life. I enjoy my work, and,
   although there are some days when I feel   SA   A   MA MD D   SD
   like staying home, I would really miss
   working if I were suddenly forced to retire.

2. Regarding work output, I feel that with-
   in certain reasonable limits I should   SA   A   MA MD D   SD
   try to produce as much as is possible.

3. Some people are always talking about
   changing jobs. While I am not totally ex-   SA   A   MA MD D   SD
   cluding that possibility, I am reason-
   ably happy where I am and I don't anticipate a change.

4. My boss is a really positive aspect of
   my job. He has his faults, like anyone
   else, but we have a good relationship,   SA   A   MA MD D   SD
   and I can go to him about anything.

5. Another strong point of my job is the
   people who work there. There are a few   SA   A   MA MD D   SD
   that I don't like a great deal, but gen-
   erally you couldn't find a nicer group
   of people to work with.

6. One of my strongest desires is to move up
   the ladder at work. Part of the success   SA   A   MA MD D   SD
   of any job is to be promoted as soon as
   possible.

7. The work that I do is really exciting and interesting. Even if I had to change jobs I SA   A   MA MD D   SD would want to continue this kind of work.

8. Regardless of my own opinion, I feel that if all the people at my place of business were polled they would not think that I am a very SA   A   MA MD D   SD efficient or effective employee. They would regard me as average or less at best.

9. The organization that I work for is an excellent example of just how fine that particular kind of organization can be. It is a success- SA   A   MA MD D   SD ful place which is well regarded by the people who know it. It does a fine job of what it does and it's a great place to work.

10. The organization that I work for is:

Very Large	Large	Medium	Small
_____	_____	_____	_____
(More than 5000 Employees)	(1000-5000 Employees)	(300-1000 Employees)	(less than 300)

11. My job could best be described as:

Executive Level	Upper Management	Middle Management	Supervisory Level	Clerical Level	Production Level
_____	_____	_____	_____	_____	_____

12. The managerial structure or climate at work might be best described as:

    _____a. Relatively rigid and military in approach.

    _____b. Although it is basically a bureaucratic or military structure, the people and procedures decrease the formality.

    _____c. Relatively informal with few levels of management.

    _____d. Very democratic with no apparent differences between individuals.

Reworded item descriptions were provided on six-point scales ranging from SA (strongly agree) to SD (strongly disagree). On all but two of the nine items shown in Exhibit 6.3, the SA response was given a quantitative value of 6 and associated with high levels of that particular variable. Other scale values, A (agree), MA (moderately agree), MD (moderately disagree), and D (disagree), were decreased by the unit value of 1 point until the value of "1" was associated with SD or low levels of the variable.

For example, Item 1 represents job satisfaction. A score of SA is scored as 6, or high job satisfaction. A score of MA would be scored 4, or slightly above average job satisfaction.

The remaining two (of nine total) items were reversed as regards their scaling. Item 3, turnover propensity, changes from SA (value of "1"), a low turnover propensity, to SD (value of 6), a high turnover propensity. Item 8, perceived image, changes from SA (value of "1"), a low image, to SD (value of 6), a high image. These steps were taken to make Study II consistent with Study I.

As in the first study, Study II attempted to gather data about six dimensions of productivity. These were:

Variable	Item Number Exhibit 6.3
y1 Job satisfaction	1
y2 Output	2
y3 Turnover propensity	3
y4 Relationship with the boss	4
y5 Relationships with coworkers	5
y6 Motivation to climb	6

In addition, the second questionnaire sought information about three variables which emerged during various discussions of the prior research.

Variable	Item Number Exhibit 6.3
y7 Satisfaction with work content	7
y8 Perceived image	8
y9 Organizational Satisfaction	9

The reverse side of the instrument sought information regarding the size of the organization where subjects were working, the level of the job (structural) and the kind of structure (autocratic versus democratic).

Subjects

Participants for the study were gathered with the assistance of SIMS Centers. First, steps were taken to insure that persons who had participated in the previous study would not be included in this second one. Then, the meditating subjects were contacted by taking instruments either to TM teaching centers or to programs such as research symposiums which were being sponsored by various SIMS Centers.

A total of 250 meditators who were also full-time workers agreed to participate in the second study. They were not asked to disclose any demographic data about themselves but they were asked to jot their relative length of meditating experience down on the top of the completed questionnaire.

The average meditating experience of this second and larger group was thirteen months, a bit longer than the average from the first study. This difference was probably due to the fact that subjects were gathered from a much broader geographic area including many big cities where TM has been popular for much longer than it had been in the original survey-center area. Subjects represented more than thirty of the fifty states plus two Canadian provinces.

The 250 nonmeditating subjects were gathered from two sources. First, 125 graduate students from Gannon College (most of these within the MBA program) were asked to fill out the research instrument. Second, 125 people with full-time jobs were also selected at random in a local shopping plaza to fill out the instrument.

The study itself, simply consisted of asking 250 meditating full-time workers and 250 nonmeditating full-time workers to complete the research instruments.

Table 6.5
The Effect of TM upon Productivity
Study II

Variable	Meditators	Nonmedi-tators	Differ-ence	Std. Error	Significance Level
y1	5.4	4.2	1.2	.28	.001
y2	5.6	4.5	1.1	.23	.001
y3	2.0	3.7	1.7	.24	.001
y4	4.9	3.6	1.3	.21	.001
y5	5.1	4.5	.6	.14	.001
y6	3.3	4.2	.9	.28	.01
y7	4.9	3.0	1.9	.31	.001
y8	5.1	4.3	.8	.25	.001
y9	3.5	3.0	.5	.14	.001

Study II: The Results

The results of the second study were assembled in Table 6.5. As in the first study the individual dimensions of productivity are symbolized by the letter y. The first six (y1 through y6) are identical to the previous productivity variables. Y7 through y9 are new dimensions which were added during Study II. A description of all of the productivity dimensions which were studied follows:

$y1$ = Job satisfaction — The general feeling which one has, either positive or negative, regarding his overall job

$y2$ = Output — The extent of or pace of work done by an employee

$y3$ = Turnover propensity — The extent to which an employee is eager to leave his company organization

$y4$ = Relationship with the boss — The quality and/or positiveness of the ongoing relationship between an employee and his supervisor

$y5$ = Relationship with coworkers — The general quality of the relationships between an individual and his fellow employees

$y6$ = Climb orientation — The extent to which an employee feels motivated to climb the organizational hierarchy

$y7$ = Job content satisfaction — The degree to which an employee enjoys the actual work that he is doing

y8 = Perceived image   — The extent to
                                 which a person
                                 feels his col-
                                 leagues at work
                                 view him as a
                                 competent and
                                 useful worker

y9 = Organizational   — The employee's
     satisfaction   perception of
                                 his own organi-
                                 zation

The results of the statistical analysis strongly supported the conclusions from the first set of studies. The meditator's answers were significantly different from those of nonmeditators, and these differences were in the same direction as the differences from Study I. The larger sample sizes which were associated with the second study provided a great deal more statistical significance than was associated with Study I. Instead of significance levels of .01 and .05, which were reported previously, the data from the second study proved to be significant at the .001 level (99.9% confidence), thus suggesting much more statistical confidence in the proposition that: "TM Improves Productivity."

The results from Table 6.5 suggest that meditators:

1. Experience a higher level of job satisfaction
2. Are more productive in terms of output criterion
3. Are less apt to want to leave their companies
4. Enjoy better relationships with their supervisors
5. Have better interpersonal relationships with their coworkers
6. Have a lower ambition to climb the organization
7. Enjoy their individual work assignments to a larger extent than nonmeditators
8. Have a better perception of their external image
9. Appear to be more highly satisfied with their own organizations

The direction and extent of the differences between meditators and nonmeditators for the first six of the nine total productivity variables are illustrated within Figures 6.3 through 6.8. Since these variables were presented and explained within the first part of the study there is no need to explain their meanings again in terms of organizational behavior. What those results, viewed in bar graph form, illustrate is that the second study strongly supported the results and interpretations which were presented before.

Since the final three variables were new to Study II, however, they will be presented individually within the next few pages.

Job-Content Satisfaction

It was clear from the first study that meditators experienced significantly higher job satisfaction on the basis of their meditating experiences than nonmeditators. There were some questions, however, regarding the component parts of this job-satisfaction variable. Did TM affect the way a person

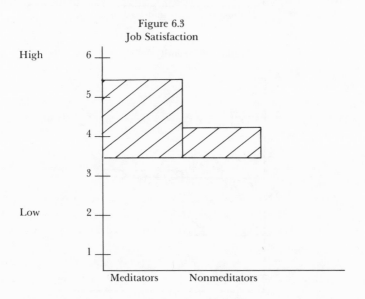

Figure 6.3
Job Satisfaction

viewed the context of his job, or the way he viewed the organization, or both?

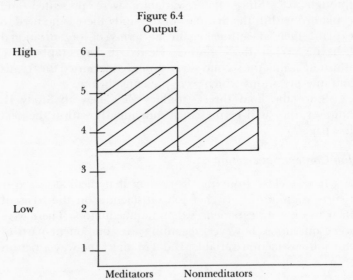

Figure 6.4
Output

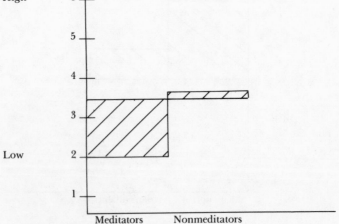

Figure 6.5
Turnover Propensity

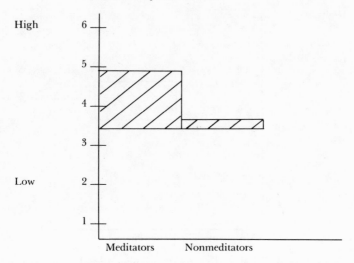

Figure 6.6
Relationship with the Boss

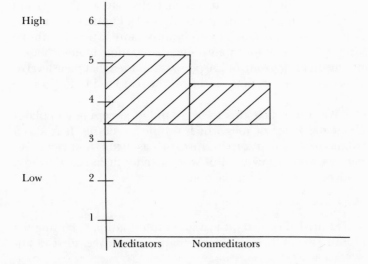

Figure 6.7
Relationships with Coworkers

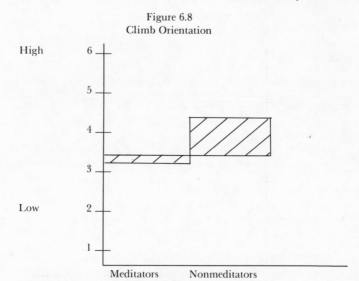

Figure 6.8
Climb Orientation

To test this issue, dimension y7 was added. Within this component of productivity we were concerned about the work content itself, not the organization, or any other aspect of the overall job.

The results of the statistical analysis between the TM and non-TM groups were quite revealing. As Figure 6.9 suggests, not only were meditators significantly more satisfied with the kind of work that they were doing than nonmeditators, but the nonmeditating group of 250 persons reported that their level of job-content satisfaction was below the zero level by half a scale point.

We might take this to be a kind of sweeping complaint about the kinds of jobs which people are doing. It is also a tribute to TM that a technique such as meditation can move persons from a low level of work-activity dissatisfaction to a moderate degree of satisfaction.

Perceived Image

Study I provided quite a lot of information regarding the overall effectiveness of the meditating employee. First of all,

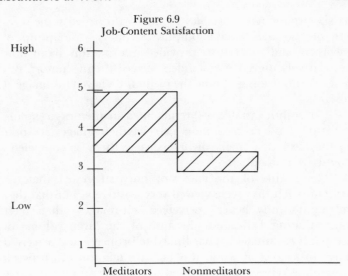

Figure 6.9
Job-Content Satisfaction

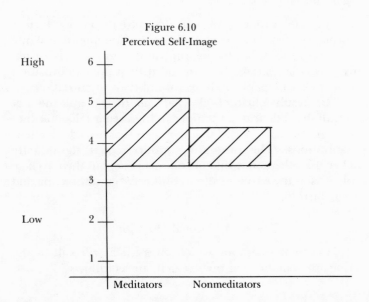

Figure 6.10
Perceived Self-Image

the six productivity variables themselves revealed some measure of the individual's output. Secondly, the group of
coworkers and supervisors provided information about how
the relatively objective bystanders viewed the meditators. But
there was no reading of how the meditator viewed his image at
work.

The eighth variable (y8) represented an attempt to explore
this issue. How do meditators perceive their images at work?
Do they feel that their coworkers view them as competent,
productive individuals?

The results of the data not only suggested that the
meditators felt they were viewed very positively, but that they
had significantly better "perceived self-images" than their
nonmeditating colleagues. Because of the large volume of
research literature which has linked self-concept and perceived
image to success at work, this positive relationship between
TM and perceived image is taken to indicate another positive
impact upon productivity.

Organizational Satisfaction

The final variable (y9) was designed to provide further
information about the general job-satisfaction question. While
y7 attempted to isolate the job content part of job satisfaction,
this particular variable was intended to supply information
about the participants' feelings toward their organizations.

The results, first of all, indicate that people do not
typically hold their organizations in high regard. Nonmeditators in particular reported that they were dissatisfied with their
organizations. The meditating group scored significantly
higher than the nonmeditators on this issue, but their average
reply was at the zero or neutral point between satisfaction and
dissatisfaction.

Some Additional Questions

Two final questions which emerged as a result of the
various presentations of my research, are as follows:

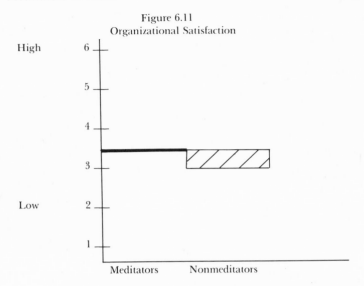

Figure 6.11
Organizational Satisfaction

1. How many people who began TM dropped the practice after some length of time?

2. What is the relationship between the length of TM experience and its impact upon various dimensions, such as productivity?

The answer to the first question comes from a second-hand report of a research project which is underway at the University of Michigan.[15] A team of researchers who are attempting to determine the rate of recidivism of the technique attempted to contact meditators in and around the Michigan area to ask if they were still practicing TM. Their findings, to date, have been that almost 70 percent of the persons who began TM are still meditating. Compared to other kinds of techniques which are oriented toward stress reduction, this 70 percent figure is fantastic.

The answer to the second question was found within the data from Study II. Part of the survey procedure was to ask each person (within the TM group) to jot down the length of his or her meditating experience. Thus, the completed questionnaires contained a measure of the length of TM experience. Due to some confusion in the instructions, however, some of the persons who participated in the study were inadvertently not asked to supply this information. Thus, from the total group of 250 meditators, only 186 supplied TM-experience data.

After reviewing the responses it seemed that a logical breaking point was one year. Thus two subgroups were formed from these 186 meditators.

1. Recent meditators—those who had been practicing TM for less than twelve full months

2. Experienced meditators—those who had been practicing TM for one year or more

Data from these two groups were broken into two sets, and the average measures for each of the productivity dimensions were recalculated. The final figures are shown in Table 6.6.

Table 6.6
The Effect of TM Experience
upon Productivity Gains

Variable	Recent Meditators	Experienced Meditators	Difference	Standard Error	Significance Level
y_1	5.2	5.6	.4	.12	.001
y_2	5.6	5.6	—	—	—
y_3	2.2	1.9	.3	.09	.001
y_4	4.6	5.3	.7	.11	.001
y_5	4.7	5.6	.9	.24	.001
y_6	3.3	3.3	—	—	—
y_7	4.3	5.0	.2	.08	.01
y_8	5.0	5.1	.1	.07	.20
y_9	3.2	3.9	.7	.05	.20

A statistical analysis of the differences between experienced and recent meditators reveals that:

The length of TM experience is positively related to the extent of the gains in productivity which are forthcoming. Experienced meditators would appear to be significantly more productive than nonmeditators.

Statistical analysis showed significant differences in several of the productivity variables. Experienced meditators reported that they:

1. Had higher levels of job satisfaction
2. Were less concerned about finding another job
3. Enjoyed better relationships with both their supervisors and coworkers
4. Felt more positive about their job content

The results also indicated significantly weak (80 percent confidence level) differences between "perceived image" and "organizational satisfaction." The other two dimensions, "output" and "ambition to climb," did not appear to be affected by the length of TM experience.

A View from Within the Nonmeditating Group

It was stated earlier that the nonmeditating group was composed of graduate students who volunteered for the study (125) and other random people (125). Part of the logic behind this design feature was to test a question which emerged regarding the control group from the first study. It was suggested that if graduate students were significantly different from average people, then the analysis of the differences between these graduate students and meditators would not be accurate. If, for example, graduate students were more productive than most people, then the differences shown in Study I would have appeared smaller than they should have.

So the productivity variables were measured separately from graduate students and for nongraduate students within the nonmeditating group. The results of a statistical analysis of the differences which were found between the two groups are shown in Table 6.7.

Table 6.7
Analysis of the Nonmeditating Group

Variable	Graduate Students	Others	Difference	Standard Error	Significance Level
y_1	4.3	4.0	.3	.16	.10
y_2	4.8	4.3	.5	.15	.001
y_3	3.8	3.7	.1	.15	none
y_4	3.7	3.5	.2	.10	.05
y_5	4.5	4.5	—	—	—
y_6	4.4	4.0	.4	.18	.05
y_7	3.2	2.8	.4	.17	.02
y_8	4.5	4.1	.4	.16	.01
y_9	3.1	2.8	.3	.08	.001

On five of the productivity dimensions used, the graduate students' scores were significantly different from the nongraduate students group. The graduate students reported that they:
1. Had a higher level of job satisfaction
2. Were more productive in terms of their output
3. Enjoyed a better relationship with their supervisors
4. Were more highly motivated to climb the organization
5. Were less dissatisfied with their work
6. Had better perceived images of themselves
7. Were less dissatisfied with their organizations
Since each of the seven significant differences which were

discovered between graduate and nongraduate students within the nonmeditating group, were in the same direction as the changes between the TM and non-TM group, it might be concluded that:

> The choice of graduate students for the control group in Study I understated the difference between the TM and control group, thus reducing the apparent magnitude of the relationship between TM and productivity.

In other words, a control group of random people during the first study may have led to greater differences in the same two groups and a stronger support for the hypothesis that TM was related to productivity.

Another Look at the First Study

The first study of TM and productivity provided some exciting insights into the relationship between stress reduction and some very important organizational dimensions. But the sample size and the design approach left some important questions about the levels of statistical significance, and more importantly the validity of the whole TM productivity hypothesis.

Study II provides additional insights into the question of TM and productivity as well as some very strong support for the conclusions which were previously presented. Having approached the same research issue with a different design and a different instrument, increases the power with which we can view the results.

It is important to note that in terms of the six variables which were presented in Study I, the second study supports each of the conclusions regarding the directions of the proposed relationships:

1. TM increases job satisfaction
2. TM improves output
3. TM reduces turnover propensity
4. TM improves the relationship with the boss
5. TM enhances relationship with coworkers
6. TM lowers motivation to climb the hierarchy

2 studies

And, since the sample size within Study II (500) was much larger than the sample size from the first study, there is a great deal more statistical confidence associated with the second set of results (99.9 percent).

Study II also added some new insights into organizational issues which were omitted within the first study. First, the job satisfaction variable was broken into its component parts—the organization versus the work itself—and, second, the perceived image of meditators was analyzed.

Finally, the design of the nonmeditating group even partly strengthened the conclusions of the first study. It suggests that the first study may have greatly understated the strength of the relationship between TM and productivity.

Implications for Management Practice

The two studies, taken together, suggest some very powerful conclusions for the managers and the participants of organizations. Beginning with the supposition that highly stressed work environments provide a major difficulty for almost every person and that TM, as it has been presented within earlier chapters, is a useful and highly efficient stress insulator, then the aggressive management of stress might include several specific steps.

General Stress Reduction—Intellectual

Since it can be shown that high levels of stress lead to greatly reduced productivity at work, companies and managers need to make every possible effort to recognize and deal with the existence of stress at least at an intellectual level. They must admit to themselves and to their employees that stress exists, and that it is unhealthy. This can begin to provide an environment where people honestly deal with a major problem, and therefore help to legitimize the desire to avoid stresses and strains at work. In this way, many of the objective stresses connnected with a particular organization can be actively dealt with and, perhaps, reduced through the cooperative efforts of managers, administrators, and employees.

But until the kind of atmosphere exists where stress is recognized as a serious threat to productivity as well as to individual well-being, this kind of stress management will not be encouraged to grow.

General Stress Reduction—Experiential

All the intellectualizations of stress, added together and multiplied by twelve, will not help the highly stressed person who is working in a stressful situation. So for the sake of the individual on the job, and the job itself, organizations should make every effort to encourage employees to engage in stress-reducing techniques. Naturally, my own recommendation would be TM, since most of the available research suggests TM to be a superefficient stress reducer. But naturally, there are other approaches to reducing stress, and some of these will be discussed in Chapter 8.

Perhaps the most important aspect of a large-scale approach to stress reduction at work is the overall sanction of the company and its employees. In other words, stress reduction must be done on a systematic basis with large-scale programs which involve many employees at different levels of the organization.

Band-Aid Stress Therapy

Since certain parts of the organization are subjected to more stress than others or than there is in the organization in general, it makes good sense to apply special preventative and therapeutic programs to these particular areas. Organizational administrators need to look for, and to treat, these high stress areas.

The research which was done previously gives some very good hints for finding high-stress areas. First, it was shown that the higher up the organization, the greater the level of stress. Second, we saw that stresses are a good deal more prominent in democratic or participative departments and organizations. So, in general, we might expect to find that executives are more highly stressed than production-level employees, and that the employees of participative groups would be more stressed than their colleagues who work in relatively autocratic environments.

Utilizing Creative Capacity

Perhaps one of the greatest paradoxes which emerge from the study of stress at work is the fact that organizations work in an upside-down problem-solving way. By this, I mean that the persons who are assigned to certain kinds of problem solutions are rendered almost helpless to solve these problems by virtue of their positions in the organization. Upper-level executives, for example, are typically asked to do creative problem solving. But the highly stressed upper atmosphere of the organization makes this difficult if not impossible. High levels of stress are not conducive to creative thinking. On the other hand the production level worker, who is shielded from stress by his position in the structure, has an incredible natural capacity for high-quality creative work which usually goes completely untapped.

So perhaps a superstrategy for organizations of all kinds would be to redirect a large percentage of the problems which require creative thinking (rather than routine or mechanical work) to lower-level participants! At the very least, these persons ought to have input into the problem-solving process. I believe, on the basis of my research and my experiences, that most companies are overlooking a huge reservoir of competent and talented problem solvers on their production floors.

Guerrilla Tactics for Organizational Warriors

Perhaps the most important step in the fight against stress starts with me! After all, if I am a highly stressed person what can I do in the big war against stress? So as selfish as it may sound, each person should first take steps to deal with stress on an individual basis. And then if the organization where he works adopts broad-based policies for reducing conflicts at work he will be just so much better off.

But for the immediate future, we must all face the realistic possibility that our organizations will not be able to eliminate a significant proportion of the stresses which surround our jobs. Consequently we must take the responsibility for our own stress management. We must find and continue to utilize a stress detoxifier, such as TM.

Although the research, to this point, strongly suggests that TM is perhaps the most powerful approach to stress reduction, there are surely other (if less efficient) approaches. We will look at some of these in Chapter 8, but first we will discuss the experiences of some companies which have begun to utilize TM on a large scale.

chapter 7

Companies That Meditate

So far we have seen a very favorable picture of TM and its impact upon both business and other kinds of organizations. In the two preceding chapters the following was shown:

1. TM has an impact upon the physiological and the psychological performance of individuals.

2. TM appears to have a positive effect upon such organizational factors as turnover, productivity, interpersonal relationships, and output.

But the research which has been developed so far has focused upon the impact of meditation on a number of individuals. Thus, the issue which remains is to learn about the impact of TM upon the overall organization where it is practiced. What happens to profit? What is the impact upon the everyday operations of the company? Although we have been exposed to a barrage of "scientific" conclusions, we must view the results in more common-sense terms. What have people who work in organizations said about their experiences with TM? And can these results be presented in ordinary (rather than scientific) language?

The purpose of this chapter is to break away from the grip of the "scientific method" and take a less formal, more anthropological trip into several organizations which have begun some kind of a systematic program of meditation. What has been the effect of TM upon the overall operation of these businesses? How have the employees reacted to the use of TM at work?

The following examples are case studies that have been extracted from the experiences of a number of companies which have begun to meditate. I hope that these aggregated experiences will help to answer many of the questions which the reader may have accumulated to this point.

The testimonials which follow have not been arranged in any particular order, but essentially fall in the chronology in which they came to me. Each company or organization is viewed from the perspective of one particular person — the person who participated in the study. Naturally, the views of these individuals are not universally held by all of their coworkers.

A few of the persons who participated in the preparation of this chapter, for reasons which were both complex and understandable, wished to remain anonymous. In these cases (which have been noted), names have been changed and the identities of the businesses are disguised.

A Small Job Shop: Electronics

The president of a southeastern Pennsylvania job shop that specializes in electronic subassembly work related his experiences with TM to me at a conference a few months ago. Mr. Smith (who wishes to remain anonymous) became interested in TM as a result of his college-age son who began meditating a few years prior to his father.

Smith's son, who works for his father on a part-time basis now and is planning to join the firm on a full-time basis after completing college, badgered Smith for months before he finally relented. Smith readily admits to trying TM just to get his son off of his back.

The results, however, went well beyond Smith's wildest expectations. As he so vividly proclaimed, "It's a shame that a great technique like TM should be wasted on kids like mine who don't need it, when most businessmen need so much help." Smith's experiences with TM were, as he put it, phenomenal. He began to sleep less, to lose weight, and to act like a reasonable person around the house. He stopped drinking, began to communicate with his family, and finally had to admit that his son was right. He needed TM.

But the greatest benefits, at least from Smith's perspective, were in his business. As the owner-operator of a job shop that had rapidly grown to more than 900 employees, Smith suddenly found himself in the midst of a situation that had almost gotten out of hand. What had started out to be a relatively modest operation, had grown to such complexity that he was not sure if he could begin to handle all the problems. And there were problems. As a job shop, Smith Company (an assumed name) had no proprietary product. Or, as Smith himself phased it, "nothing to count on . . . no stability."

Life at Smith Company was hectic to say the least. Products were being phased in and out. Production lines were constantly being torn down and rebuilt, sales and production quotas vacillated wildly from month to month. But perhaps the major problem was in management. Smith recognized the need to attract and keep a small staff of competent management personnel, but he was experiencing some tremendous turnover problems.

It seemed that every time a new man got to the point where he was producing at his job, he would quit and go to another company. As Mr. Smith was later to find out, that problem came from the top. Because he reacted so violently to the changing conditions of his business and he had such a feeling of helplessness about his own job, Mr. Smith had become impossible to work with. He was given to yelling at people, humiliating them in front of their colleagues, and not listening to their advice. Worse yet, he was inconsistent. One day he would praise and compliment a worker. On the next, he would do the opposite.

TM made Smith a nice boss. In fact the impact of the technique was so strong and so immediate that his management staff noticed it almost immediately. On the third or fourth working day one of his closest associates came into Smith's office and said, "Well, all right, why don't you tell me about it? Did you sell the business or merge with someone or what?" Smith's behavior had changed so dramatically (for the better) that the people around him were worried at first.

Smith Company is now a much better place to work. Smith offers to pay some of the price of TM training for any employee who is interested. And at last count, nine of the top fifteen staff members are meditating. According to Smith, the turnover problem has ceased to exist, overtime work has been radically reduced, and the business is stronger than ever in terms of sales orders and its financial position.

Smith, for the first time since beginning his business, has developed a kind of fundamental confidence that the place can function without him. As a matter of fact, he is planning his first long-term vacation.

A Diversified Machinery Manufacturing Group

One of the most outspoken advocates of TM (in terms of his personal business experiences) is William Hickey, the young and energetic president of Gear Technologies, Inc., of Bloomfield, Connecticut. Hickey's success story began in the very same place where many success stories ended — with the decline of the aerospace industry. Beginning like many other engineers, a displaced technocrat in search of a new vocation, Hickey seized upon the idea of going into business for himself. Then, armed with the benefits of TM, a new-found technique, Hickey and his partner, Jerome Elbaum, simply built an eleven-company conglomerate boasting international sales which exceed $10 million per year and with 400 employees.

Hickey attributes much of his instant success to TM. He states that he was very skeptical of meditation at the beginning of his experiences with the technique. But as he continued to meditate, he began to notice clear indications of its impact upon him. Associates at work were amazed by his calmness. They, more than anything else, made him aware of the extent to which he had changed. Hickey also reported that since TM he has found more and more time to spend with his wife and children.

Citing his company as an extremely volatile and highly paced enterprise, Hickey praises the impact of TM on his colleagues at work. (He strongly encourages his employees to learn TM.) He feels that TM is particularly useful to a dynamic firm because of its facility to help people adapt to stressful situations. His secretary, who is also a meditator, is a good example of a person who can easily deal with turmoil without adverse effect. And as Hickey says, "Without her tranquility and capacity to make sense of otherwise trying situations, her job would be impossible."

A Post-Secondary Trade School

Bob Annechario is not the kind of guy whom, in a crowded hotel lobby, you would tab as a company president. Instead, he looks like he could be the moderator of a TV talk show or perhaps a super salesman. But Annechario is, in fact, a young man with a very impressive list of accomplishments. He is a well-known metal sculptor and a recognized expert in the field of nuclear welding. But more importantly (for our purposes at least), he is the dynamic young president of Creative Metals, Inc., the first post-secondary trade school in New England.

Creative Metals, while a kind of educational organization, is, in reality, a profit-making organization. As such, it is in the business of exchanging tuition dollars for the opportunity to learn a very exacting and lucrative skill — nuclear welding. Young people come to Creative Metals, pay a very substantial training fee, and then enter into training programs in order to learn the intricacies of nuclear welding.

Creative Metals has a dual involvement with TM. First, Annechario and a number of his staff members have learned to meditate. He attributes much of his great success in his business to his TM experience, and further demonstrates his enthusiasm for meditation by offering to pay for any staff member who wants to learn the technique. But a second and more potentially important involvement of Creative Metals involves TM and the students at the school.

One of Annechario's business problems was expanding the number of students fast enough to fulfill the critical demands for nuclear welding. Prompted by this and the corresponding problems of unemployment, Bob hit upon the idea of trying to train "previously unemployable persons" in the rigorous skills of nuclear welding, by training them in TM at the same time. Two major obstacles were successfully overcome enroute to Creative Metals' new training program. First, the state of Connecticut was prevailed upon to provide funds for the project and to supply lists of eligible trainees. Second, the Maharishi was asked to help design a specific meditation program which would minister to the specialized needs of this task.

The problem here is first to take persons who have traditionally been categorized as "unemployable" and to moti-vate them to learn this complex skill. Clearly, the reason for the existence of the unemployable person in the first place is often related to the fact that he or she can't get a job which pays sufficiently more than the aggregate benefits of not working. In this instance, Annechario would seem to have, at least, a fighting chance, since nuclear welding is a very lucrative field. But beyond this preliminary problem, there is the monumental task of the training itself. Can such a hard-core unemployable group be trained to perform in such a complex and difficult task? The experiences of many experts would suggest that this is a kind of fruitless venture, that such a strong pattern of failure has been set up through the life experiences of these people, that the chances of their being able to learn such an intricate pattern of skills are remote at best.

But Annechario is not discouraged. He feels that his specially designed program of TM will facilitate learning skills among his new students, and that by working a schedule of meditation into the training routines of the students, his faculty will be able to successfully teach the complexities of welding to this group.

Several different aspects of this project make it a highly unique situation. First, this is one of the very few applications where TM will be imposed upon people. Any person entering the program under the state subsidy will be required to integrate TM with his technical training. Second, there are several sophisticated and scientific attempts of measurements being taken of the ongoing process. Annechario's staff has established normal times for training on the basis of their previous experience with students. Finally, a control group of "unemployables" minus TM training has been processed through the school.

When the results of this study emerge, there will be some very powerful data relating to TM and productivity, at least in regard to the training function itself.

A Management Consulting Firm

Perhaps the most outspoken advocate of TM in the business world is Michael Dawson, an associate of Arthur D. Little, the internationally known consulting company. Dawson's experiences with TM come from both his personal practice of the technique and the fact that thirty of his colleagues have also begun the technique.

As you might guess, the management-consulting business is even more changeable and exciting than most other organizational climates. This is particularly true of A.D.L. because of the nature and scope of the assignments that they take on. Arthur D. Little has consulted to relatively large companies in much the same way that smaller or less ambitious firms might take on a medium-sized company. The overall impact of this scope of operations is twofold. In terms of the consulting industry, A.D.L. has gained the reputation of being the Rolls Royce of consultants. But for the employees, especially the consultants themselves, the result is possibly a bit more negative. The job environment of this type of organization must, by necessity, be so complex and dynamic that employees are subject to an incredible volume of stress.

Dawson, recognizing the stressful environment within which he was working, realized his own need for a stress-reducing tool. Thus he was drawn to TM and found that the benefits of the technique greatly enhanced his performance at work. Perhaps the greatest benefit which he found was the increased capacity he developed for understanding and dealing with people. And in his particular business that talent was critical for, as he put it, most of the really difficult people were clients, not coworkers.

But the more interesting aspects of Dawson's experiences with TM come from the increase in the use of the technique by other employees of A.D.L. It might have been the changes that they saw in Dawson, or perhaps it was simply that they were driven by their highly stressed work environments, but, in any case, a rather large group of persons from A.D.L. began to practice TM. From Dawson's perspective the results were rather amazing. Suddenly the projects were flowing more smoothly through the office, the employees were getting along much better, and a kind of positive atmosphere was developed where people became aware of the stresses and strains of their jobs and tried to help each other deal with problems in a reinforcing way. One of the unique aspects of the A.D.L. experience is that the meditating employees were able to set aside a special room for TM, and to work their individual practices of TM into their daily schedules.

Dawson tells of the experiences of one particular meditating management consultant in the following way. One of the most aggressive and successful of A.D.L.'s people was a relatively young man who suddenly — and quite unexpectedly

— suffered a heart attack. When this fellow returned to work after a moderate period of rest and recuperation, he had a great deal of difficulty getting back into the swing of things. His cardiologist had advised him of the dangers of working in a highly stressful job environment and, consequently, he was afraid to really get immersed in the job to the extent that he had been. But by the same token he was not at all satisfied with a low-key approach to work. He wanted to dive back into his profession, but he was afraid to.

One day this particular man called Dawson and asked him if he thought that TM might help his particular situation. When Dawson told him of the impact of TM upon stress and upon cardiovascular well-being he immediately decided to try it. The effects of TM upon the productivity of this individual were phenomenal. After just a few months of meditating, he was doing more work than ever before, and doing it with less energy.

Overall Dawson reports that the A.D.L. experience with TM has been very positive. Although all of the examples have not been quite so dramatic as the one just given, almost everyone who began to meditate has found the practice has a positive effect upon his or her work performance. Dawson feels that TM has a great potential for the consulting industry as well as other rapidly changing areas.

A Medical Packaging Organization

Chairman of the Board Rick Polk reports one of the most comprehensive cases of the practice of TM among managers of a large corporation. P.A. Medical Corporation, in its two different divisions in two states, has so encouraged the practice of TM that 50 percent of the administrative staff of one plant and 100 percent of the other are active meditators.

Polk heartily endorses the benefits of meditation for his enterprise. In a letter written to Daniel Kaufman, president of the American Foundation for the Science of Creative Intelligence, he writes:

. . . I have less tension and stress and greater clarity of mind enabling me to make more effective and intelligent decisions. Responsibilities which before I felt only I could handle, I am now able to share more creatively and harmoniously with my executives and employees.

. . . We have found that the executives and the employees are working together more effectively and accomplishing greater productivity with significantly decreased absenteeism. The general atmosphere of the plant has markedly improved and the working conditions seem to be more pleasant and acceptable.

I heartily recommend TM to the executives of those companies wishing greater productivity as a result of increased energy and efficiency from those employees practicing TM.

Mr. Polk's experiences suggest that the benefits of TM to the organization may be linked to the percentage of persons who are practicing the technique.

A Public Accounting Firm

Mr. Brown (not his real name) is a partner in one of Canada's most prosperous public accounting firms. In fact the level of his firm's prosperity was so great that it was leading to the slow but steady destruction of Brown himself.

Brown characterized his business as "crazy." His accounting firm had become increasingly involved in work with firms which had government contracts. And as Brown himself admitted "the complexity and volume of the accounting red tape which is associated with government work in Canada has become mind-boggling." The public accountant is placed in the unenviable position of interpreting points of law and translating them into sound accounting practice. Then, to make things worse, he must take total responsibility for any errors in judgment.

Mr. Brown related to me that he had reached a kind of breaking point at work. He could no longer digest the volumes of rules and regulations which were flowing through his firm quickly enough to do a substantial volume of accounting work. Consequently he was both losing business which he couldn't get to, and doing a bad job on the work that he was doing.

His home life was a reflection of his business problems. He would go home late each night, eat dinner, sit down in front of the TV with an armful of papers or documents to read, and promptly fall asleep.

But then he was exposed to TM, and in just a few weeks his entire approach to work changed. He was suddenly able to digest the volumes of rules and regulations which were passing through his desk-top organizer. As he put it, he changed from a fifty-year-old accountant who felt like it was time to retire because he couldn't keep up, to a fifty-year-old accountant who felt like he was thirty.

The results of Brown's TM experiences soon became apparent in his organization as well. His accounting productivity picked up. In addition, he became so adept at digesting and understanding the new accounting practices which were being requested by the government, that he began to do workshops for his partners and junior accountants. This resulted in a significant increase in their output as well.

Today his business could be characterized as extremely successful. A number of his colleagues have begun TM, his secretary is a meditator, and, while the volume of work has increased, the pace has become more relaxed. The firm is doing twice as much work as it used to in two-thirds of the time.

A Large Commercial Bank

The personnel officer of Upper Avenue National Bank, a highly successful banking operation in Chicago, reports the results of TM at the bank to be very favorable. After meditating for more than a year, she states that "it would take a lot to make me stop TM."

Lauretta Cesario and a dozen officials of the bank began TM at approximately the same time. The meditators, approximately ten percent of the management staff of the bank, included the president and at least two vice-presidents. Lau-

retta has experienced many changes in her own job performance since TM. Her major observation is that she had noticed
an increased "awareness" or, as she puts it, an ability to see
herself as separated from the various impacts of what she is
doing. She views herself as more productive, more efficient,
much more energetic, and better in her dealings with the
people around her.

Ms. Cesario views the major impact of TM at her place of
business in terms of interpersonal relationships. Many of the
people who have begun to meditate are now much smoother in
their dealings with the people around them. One person in
particular, a supervisor, has made dramatic improvements in
her capacity to relate not only with her subordinates but with
the people around her as well.

TM would appear to hold great promise for the entire
financial industry, a traditionally volatile place to work.

A Machine Shop

Perhaps one of the most systematic and thorough
applications of TM in a work setting comes from the King (an
assumed name) Machine Works which is located in West
Germany. The son of the family which controls the business
was exposed to TM as a student in the United States. And he
was so taken by the technique and its potential for improving
productivity at work, that he returned to Germany after
graduation with a strong conviction to apply TM to his future
place of business.

Naturally his first major task was to convince his father,
the operating executive of the factory, of the merits of TM. His
approach was a simple one. He talked his father into beginning the practice of meditation. And after a few weeks of TM,
his father was even more enthusiastic than he was about the
large potential for TM at work.

A program of TM was offered to any employee who was
interested, and the company picked up a large percent of the
costs. As a result of the owner's infectious enthusiasm for TM,
almost all of the employees of the company agreed to take part

in this program of employee revitalization. But an even more unique aspect of this particular company's approach to TM is that the employees are encouraged to meditate on company time. The typical pattern of work consists of a twenty-minute meditation break in both the morning and the afternoon.

After a period of more than one year, King Machine Works reports that its productivity has shown a slow but steady rise. Naturally the productivity figures included the loss of forty minutes per day of meditating time. Thus individual efficiency was so greatly facilitated by the implementation of TM that workers were easily able to compensate for their lost meditating time through their improved productivity.

The people at this family-owned business are more than pleased with their TM experience. The workers find their jobs to be more rewarding, and also more financially lucrative (since they are working on incentive standards). And the management finds that its relationship with its work force has improved substantially. This is perhaps due to the common experience of TM, which both management and the work force can relate to. And the final bonus is that productivity has increased very dramatically, thus strengthening the company's competitive position.

A Professional Football Team

What better application for a productivity increasing tool could there be than a modern professional football team? On the continuum of work we find today's professional teams far from the sport-loving beer-drinking players of a century ago. As a matter of fact, professional football has become such a large-scale business that it is beginning to resemble the corporate monolith more than just a simple game. Problems of negotiations, marketing, and business practices underlie most of the major team franchises.

As a result of the rapidly increasing levels of both competition and complexity within the game of football, the levels of stress which players are subjected to have increased dramatically within the last few years. Individual players find that they are not able to play as well as they should, because of vastly increasing anxiety. Perhaps, then, football — at least professional football — represents a prime application for a technique such as TM.

The September 23, 1974, edition of the *New York Post* featured an article entitled "These Four Jets Are Meditating," which represents one of the first reports of a systematic attempt by a football team to improve its performance via the reduction of stress. Actually the Jets' approach to TM is not systematic in the sense of being encouraged or run by team officials. It would seem that the team's outspoken quarterback, Joe Namath, is providing the major impetus for the spread of the technique among team members. Namath learned about TM from Bob Oates, Jr. who coauthored his latest book. And, after trying the technique, he was so impressed with it and convinced that it would help his game, he talked to teammates about it during the preseason training camp. Namath's preseason, perhaps a leading indicator of the effect of TM upon football productivity, was his best since playing professional football.

Four members of the Jets, including Namath, flanker Eddie Bell, tackle Bob Shivus, and quarterback Al Woodall, are now meditating. Six other team members are waiting to begin meditating, and a number of the other players are said to be very interested. Perhaps the kind of season that the Jets have will be improved by the reduction of player stress. The idea seems to make a lot of sense to the players, and the coach certainly hopes that they are right.

The United States Army

At the beginning of this section, it was suggested that TM has been utilized with some success in many different kinds of organizations. For some people, the U.S. Army will seem the most unique of all. But actually the military, which began as the model for business organization, continues to exist as a major place of employment in this and many other countries. So naturally it suffers from all of the trials and tribulations of any other major employer.

Perhaps the most notable TMer in the Army is Major General Franklin M. Davis, Commandant of the Army War College in Carlisle, Pennsylvania. His active endorsement of TM has caused meditation to become quite popular in the service. Classes have been held on several different army posts, including Fort Bliss and Fort Dix. General Davis claims that TM has helped him to be a more effective administrator by allowing him to become calmer and more relaxed. He reports that his blood pressure has been lowered by ten points since meditating.

One of the first major usages of TM within the Army has been to combat drug addiction, one of the Army's most nagging problems. The Pentagon's Alcohol and Drug Policy Division head, Colonel Leslie R. Fornery, has announced the voluntary use of TM within various drug-abuse programs.

While the Army is being cautious about making an early or a blanket endorsement of TM, the indications are that in certain areas of the organization, there is a great deal of enthusiasm.

A Dairy Company

I met Stan Eisenberg, the president of Sunny Dale Farms, at a symposium in New York City for the reduction of stress in business and industry. He immediately struck me as a highly efficient and competent young man. His business, the consumer food industry, is a highly complex and changing one.

Stan's experiences with TM were, from his own perspective, superpositive. He related to me the general conditions of his industry, as well as the kinds of stresses and strains that he faces on a day-to-day basis, as the president of such a complex and dynamic enterprise. Perhaps one of the most difficult aspects of executive life for Eisenberg, was the problem of traveling. His particular business and life styles include at least two transcontinental flights per week. And as anyone who has tried that kind of a schedule soon finds out, the time changes, the rushing, the waiting in airport terminals, and the general trip anxieties soon exact a great toll on the traveler.

The effect of TM on Eisenberg was to soften the impact of his stressful style of living and working. He reported that after a few weeks of TM he was able to sleep less, he became less irritable, and he began to have more fun at his job.

Seeing the effects of TM upon himself, and the added benefits in terms of his job, made Eisenberg begin to promote the use of TM for his employees. The last time that I talked to him he had encouraged a large number of his top-level managers to begin the technique, and was beginning, as he put it, to enjoy the benefits of better working relationships, increased productivity, and better decisions at work. In fact, his only problem seemed to revolve about the development of better ways for convincing members of his staff to try it.

A Large Insurance Company

Connecticut General Life Insurance Company is experimenting with TM. While there is no formally launched program of TM being implemented at this major eastern insurance company, enough top-level personnel have expressed an interest in the application of TM to the problems of doing business at Connecticut General to prompt training director, Richard Miller, to begin an experimental investigation.

Miller reports that his company's approach to employee development is not rigid or structured like the programs in many similarly sized organizations. Instead, Connecticut General attempts to match programs of development with individual employees. Thus, the company-supported program for one employee may be radically different from the program for a second or third individual. In keeping with this flexible development program, Connecticut General does not endorse any particular educational or personal-development strategy.

The TM experiment, like many other programs within the flexible framework at Connecticut General, began on an ad-hoc basis. A few of the managers who had been exposed to the notions of stress release and TM decided that they should approach their company with the idea of absorbing the training costs. And because of the substantial volume of research data pointing to the positive relationship between TM and productivity, the company decided to begin a small-scale experiment.

At this time, only a dozen employees (five of whom began with their wives) have been trained in the technique. And as Miller put it, "Twelve in 12,000 isn't going to make for impressive statistics." But, from talking to five of the men who are involved in the program, at least one thing is clear: they are enjoying the experience. Not one of them reports any kind of a negative experience associated with TM. In fact, most of them report that their meditating experience has helped them to become more productive and to enjoy their jobs a lot more.

Before any grand conclusions can be drawn from the Connecticut General experience, much more time will have to pass and much more data will have to be collected. In fact, the whole notion of the application of a single technique such as TM to a large and dynamic organization such as this one may be extremely tenuous. Perhaps the very size and complexity of a place like Connecticut General dictates against the wholesale application of one singular program. We might wonder if the systematic application of TM in a company will have to be associated with a place which is significantly smaller than Connecticut General.

In Conclusion

We have seen the assembled experiences of several different kinds of companies and organizations within this chapter. Taken by itself, this kind of a series of testimonials, no matter how positive, or how long, should not provide the kind of support which would allow a skeptic or a scientific model builder to accept the existence of a strong positive relationship between TM and productivity. But these experiences of practicing managers who have attempted to utilize TM for the management of stress, taken in the context of the data from Chapter Two, add power to the previous conclusions. It would seem that the practical experiences of the large numbers of people who have tried to utilize TM at their jobs more than substantiate the theoretical predictions that TM would increase productivity.

It is clear, however, that this particular assemblage of organizations does not represent a cross section of American business and industry. In fact, most of the accounts of TM and work which have been included within this chapter are unique at least in terms of size. Almost every account of a company which has successfully utilized TM in some form comes from either a small or a medium-sized firm. Does this mean that TM is not appplicable to a large firm? I don't think so. But it would seem to me that the chances of a large company beginning the systematic application of a technique such as TM are remote at best. The one common ingredient in all of the medium or small companies which have adopted programs of TM appears to be a highly motivated upper-level employee who becomes enthralled by the technique, and then devotes much of his energy to having his employees try it. Perhaps the complex political realities of the typical large company preclude this happening. In a large enough company or organization, it would seem that you can suggest anything, and at least one high-level official will be against it.

Surely this does not indicate that the use of TM should or will be limited to small or medium-sized business firms. It does suggest, however, that the broad application to major industrial concerns is at least a few years away. In the meantime, those of us who continue to work in these large firms must provide for the management of our own stress.

The question of how to conduct a sensible program of stress management continues to be a very difficult one, particularly in companies which are either sufficiently large or particularly resistant to notions such as TM. To a large extent, each one of us must survey our individual situation, and try to come up with a plan for recognizing and dealing with stress at work. And also, as our interests begin to move from the application of stress management to ourselves toward the application of stress-reducing techniques for our colleagues or our subordinates, then we must begin to explore the realistic possibility that TM or any other single technique may not be universally acceptable. We must begin to include in our systematic programs of stress management, a variety of approaches for stress reduction.

But, what are some of these other approaches to stress reduction? And how can they be applied to the management of stress at work? These are some of the issues which will be dealt with in the next chapter.

chapter 8

Other Approaches to Stress Release

While much of the book, so far, has addressed itself to TM, a technique for the reduction of stress, it was not an interest in TM itself which motivated the writing of this book, but rather the study of stress at work. The first step, at the beginning of the book, was a discussion of the general problems of stress at work. It was suggested that highly stressed workers at all organization levels were becoming the norm rather than the exception. The second major step within the book was to present and then describe stress in terms of its impact on the individual as well as the job. The remainder of the book has attempted to investigate the impact and the value of stress reduction upon working people in terms of both their job performance and their personal lives. TM was taken, due to the large and substantial body of research literature associated with it, to be a highly efficient stress-reducing technique. Thus,

the major question so far has been this: How does the reduction of stress affect the individual at his job? And the answers
would appear to be very encouraging. Persons whose stress
levels are reduced appear to be significantly more productive
and satisfied than those who are highly stressed.

As a technique TM appears to be a highly sensitive and
powerful tool. But it is equally clear that the benefits of TM are
operating in very individual ways. Consequently, this study
is not oriented toward making generalizations about TM.
And while my own opinion after being involved within this
research project for almost two years is that TM is potentially
the most important and beneficial technique that I have ever
encountered, I am not justified in making that statement from
the perspective of a scientist. I can conclude, however, that

> TM reduces stress and that the corresponding reduction
> in stress levels is associated with increased productivity
> and efficiency at work. People who operate at relatively
> low levels of stress apprear to enjoy their work, to get
> along better with other people, and to be more effective at
> their jobs.

Since the focus of this book is the reduction of stress, and
not the integrity of a particular technique, it would seem
useful to deal with other ways for stress reduction. Surely the
practice of Transcendental Meditation is not the only way
toward reduced levels of stress. There are many thousands of
persons working productively and at corresponding low levels
of stress who have never heard of TM or, for that matter, of
stress. What kinds of techniques do these persons employ?
How can they escape the problems which assail most of the rest
of us? Are there other techniques for stress reduction?

My research suggests a number of other kinds of
techniques or approaches which show promise in the reduction of stress. And the purpose of this chapter will be to present
them and discuss their potential impact upon stress reduction
and productivity. We will begin the section with an overview
of techniques which are clearly related to organizational
behavior such as sensitivity training, MBO, and transactional
analysis. From here the discussion will move toward less

organizationally oriented approaches such as exercise programs, yoga, and religious experiences.

The Personality Versus Stress

Before addressing any specific techniques for the reduction of stress, however, it is important to discuss the impact of the personality type upon this entire issue. These questions of "what is a stressful situation?" and "to what extent is stress absorbed by an individual?" are clearly very personal and changeable constructs. So that what would be an enormously stressful situation for one person may prove to be almost a pleasant experience for the next. It is clear that some of us are much better adapted to stressful situations than others.

Each of us has a unique physiological and psychological framework from which we operate. The result is that as we step off into the complex world filled with its many kinds of stresses, our own personal environment begins to be loaded down with potential stressors. The question of who becomes highly stressed must then be mediated by at least two factors: (1) the state of the environment, and (2) the individual framework of the person.

It would seem that many of us chance into either highly stressful environments or the opposite. Perhaps it is also possible that some of us exercise subtle emotional needs to either avoid or to challenge stress by making certain kinds of occupational or vocational choices. The medical doctor who chooses a particular kind of surgical specialty, for example, may be exposing himself to significantly more stress than his colleague who decides upon a general practice. Thus, the first indications of how much stress a person will be exposed to on a daily basis and then accumulate over time are strongly related to the kinds of situations where he places himself.

The second, and perhaps more important, criterion for determining the extent to which a person becomes stressed is his — for lack of a better term — personality. In Chapter 4 it is shown that some persons are just naturally less affected by stresses than others. They seem to have a capacity for dealing calmly with the most difficult of situations.

In terms of stress management then, perhaps the most fundamental of all techniques, even though this might not actually qualify as a technique, is to avoid stressful situations and to practice the art of tranquility or relaxation. The difficulty with this kind of advice, however, is that there is no set of operational instructions. I have no clear-cut rules for changing a personality. Nor can I make simple suggestions for those who don't want to change to calmer or less stressful occupations.

Neither do I mean to imply that the calmest and most stress-avoiding type of persons could not use an external technique such as TM for the reduction of stress. It would seem that all of us are subjected to more stressful situations than we should be expected to be able to cope with. But it is just as obvious that the differences in these situations as well as the great differences in people account for much disparity in the apparent levels of stress around us.

Organizational Development

Since the Hawthorne studies of the late 1930's, the extent and scope of interest in the plight of the individual at the organization has mushroomed. While much of the early work was crude, at best, in terms of its behavioral and organizational sophistication, a broad spectrum of contemporary tools has grown out of the human-relations movement. Many of these approaches have now been grouped within a broad category of techniques which are designed to encourage the acquisition and development of interpersonal skills.

Sensitivity Training

Perhaps the most famous (or infamous depending upon your perspective) of these techniques is sensitivity (or T-group) training. While sensitivity training is complex and difficult to define, as it is a highly personal experience for each person who undergoes it, the following incomplete definition is offered:

Sensitivity training is moderated interpersonal experience oriented towards helping one to gain an increasing awareness of who he is, what his needs are, how his behavior affects those around him, and how to recognize the existence and needs of others.

Since the beginnings of sensitivity training in 1948, the literature has grown quite dramatically. And while the early reports of T-groups were superpositive in terms of the reported results upon persons who participated and their organizations, later research has been very much split in terms of its overall opinion. While some writers continue their glowing reports, others are suggesting that T-groups may be dysfunctional either to the participants or to their organizations, or to both.

Perhaps there is no other single training tool which has attracted such a violently different array of opinions from the experts. And in the past few years, contingency theory and other management developments have emerged which may begin to explain some of the essential problems with the variable impact of T-groups.

First, it would seem that there are some persons who benefit much more from T-groups than others. Why does this happen? How can it be explained? Recent research suggests that sensitivity training represents a very supportive experience for those of us who are democratic or person-oriented. But for the opposite kind of individual, the task-oriented autocrat, T-groups are potentially destructive and frustrating. The autocratic person may enter into a T-group in a most objective way, hoping to learn or gain from his experience. But he is likely to find the totally democratic environment which usually prevails within a T-group to be increasingly difficult to cope with. His reaction to this situation is quite likely to be an interpretation of failure on his own part. In other words, since T-groups are supposed to be a training in interpersonal process, and yet the experience itself is not a positive one, a person may be tempted to conclude that he is a failure. But there is every evidence that the autocratic person can do a very competent job of leadership given the right situation. Therefore, T-groups may be completely dysfunctional for all but the most democratic individuals.

A second fundamental problem with the T-group is related to the parent organizations of its participants. Since sensitivity training is a prototype for democratic structure, it follows in logic that the training experiences can only be useful within democratic environments. Thus if participants from autocratic organizations are exposed to a training experience that suggests that the organizations which sent them are not structured correctly, then either the trainees will be frustrated when they return to their jobs, or they will have to reject the new training. In either case, the value of the training is suspect. This is particularly true in light of our understanding of the usefulness of autocratic organizational structures for many kinds of tasks.

The third and final problem with T-group training arises from its bad reputation. Probably most of this is not deserved but the past few years have seen such a dramatic increase in the numbers and kinds of training groups which claim to be doing sensitivity training that many managers view T-group training in the wrong light. Managers wonder, and with good reason, if the money that they spend for sensitivity training is going to provide a real learning experience that is related to the job, or if trainees might not end up spending a weekend floating nude in a body temperature swimming pool. In short, there is a substantial problem about the definition of T-group training itself. And this is particularly true for managers and other working persons who are removed from the various professions of the behavioral sciences.

The fact remains, however, that T-group training can be a very useful and efficient approach to stress reduction at the level of the organization or at the level of the individual. Taking the large-scale changes toward an increasingly complex work environment and the corollary adjustments of organizations toward democratic structure, the amount of pressure placed upon the people in those organizations is very great. Participants, who for the most part have been raised and trained within relatively autocratic organizations, need to develop skills in democratic process. T-group training, when attempted by persons who are relatively comfortable with a democratic approach, can be a powerful tool for understanding and utilizing the interpersonal skills which are so vitally needed within participative work groups. Thus the people who receive this kind of sophistication may be able to bring a kind of new understanding to their jobs which will help them to adapt to situations that had previously caused a great deal of stress.

Organizational Development Training

Because of the highly personal nature of sensitivity training and more particularly the remote connections with the reality of organizational goals, many people became disenchanted with the T-group approach. Many examples of dysfunctional T-groups were cited in early literature. One common syndrome was for a relatively task-oriented organization to place its employees in a kind of sensitivity training double bind. First they would send an employee off for human-relations training. The effect of the training experience would be to convince the employee that he needed to expand and develop his human-relations skills. So the newly enthusiastic employee returns to the job eager to practice his newly developed potencies. But he finds the same old organization that he left. In fact, it may now seem much more autocratic than ever before. The employee soon begins to sense a major dilemma. Why did they send me for this training if they didn't want me to use it? His natural reaction is to be frustrated and disappointed with his job. He may even reach the point where he decides to quit and look for a new job which will allow him to practice his sensitivity-training skills.

OD has evolved within the past few years in an effort to link the major advantages of these behavioral skills with the needs of the organization itself. It might best be defined as sensitivity training in context, or T-groups which focus upon the organization and its goals.

A large number of companies, both large and small, have begun programs of organizational development for their employees. The results of these programs show great promise for improving the positions of both the organizations and their personnel. Many OD programs begin with, or at least include, sensitivity-training experiences. But the fundamental difference remains within the ongoing existence of OD groups at the company. Persons are not left alone in their organizations trying to practice their newly acquired skills. Instead they have the continuing feedback of colleagues who are in the same "fix," so to speak. Also, OD focuses in on the goals of the organization. Thus the OD group, which could also be a working department, might find itself meeting, from time to time, to duscuss the interpersonal and the technical problems involved in their goal accomplishment.

So OD, even more than sensitivity training, can be very useful in helping persons gain an awareness of what is going on around them at work. The OD group may have a very useful influence in the reduction of stress at work.

Management by Objectives

Management by Objectives, or MBO as it is popularly described, goes one step beyond OD in dealing with the problems of the organization. Instead of focusing primarily upon the human-relations aspects of an organization or, more particularly, the persons who work there, MBO takes a macroscopic approach. It asks fundamental questions about what the organization is doing, or where it is going, and then it attempts to build an integral approach to the acccomplishment of these goals.

The MBO approach was pioneered by Peter Drucker[1] whose early work entitled *The Practice of Management* was both popular and well-received among managers. Drucker's prescription was that each executive and manager, from lowest to highest levels, should have clear objectives which reflect the goals of the organization. These objectives must be interconnected so that different goals from the various levels of the organization would mesh together to form a highly efficient master plan.

Carroll and Tosi[2] list the following five elements for an effective MBO program in their recent book, *Management by Objectives: Applications and Research:*

1. Effective goal-setting and planning by top levels of the management hierarchy.
2. Organizational commitment to the approach.
3. Mutual goal-setting.
4. Frequent performance review.
5. Some degree of freedom in developing means for the achievement of objectives.

In summary, an MBO program is a very broad-based approach to planning, organizing, and evaluating an organization. It emphasizes participation; at least at the level of the management team. Thus it carries with it the corollary advantages of building employees who feel that they are a part of their job and that they have been involved in policy-making decisions at least for their own work units.

MBO also works at the micro-organizational level, that is, the place where individuals interact with each other and with their jobs. The basic approach of MBO, which is to establish and to articulate nesting sets of organizational goals, makes a good deal of sense for improving the general quality of work for each individual. Objective goals for sections may be factored into goals for departments and then for individuals. And the simple existence of these goals along with the process of encouraging participants to get involved in the goal-setting process, provides a more objective platform for the interpretation of behavior throughout the organization. Performance and performance standards can be both internalized and clarified via the MBO process.

Again, the systemization of organizational goals and process can greatly assist in the reduction of stresses which are caused by the organization. The MBO program helps employees understand and come to grips with the realities of organizational life.

Transactional Analysis

Transactional analysis, or TA as it is popularly referred to, is a very useful technique for dissecting and evaluating complex interpersonal relationships. The proper use of TA can greatly improve the quality of our relationships by helping us to unravel the difficulties caused by differences in our interpersonal approaches.

Each of us has probably experienced the kind of situation where we emerge from a verbal encounter with another person feeling confused or bewildered by what has just happened. TA suggests that many of these interpersonal dilemmas can be understood by viewing the persons involved as having three different ego states:

The parent — who judges, controls, manipulates, and remains in charge

The adult — who is logical, scientific, calculating, data processor, and mediator of the other ego states

The child — who is the impetuous, fun-loving, and emotional part of the personality

TA suggests that while each of us has the inherent capacity to behave from each of these individual ego states, we also have a basic style. One person might lean toward his "adult" while another seems to favor his "child" or his "parent." And many of the difficulties within interpersonal processes (transactions) come from the existence of dissimilar ego states between participants, and the kinds of defense mechanisms which naturally follow.

The boss walks into a subordinate's office, for example, and says, "Where is the project that you were supposed to have done this morning?" The employee stammers ". . . ah . . . gee, sir, I tries my best but I just couldn't . . ." "No excuses," exclaims the boss, "what I want is a result, not an excuse!" "But, sir, there were a lot of tricky little parts of this project that I had to work very hard on and it wasn't my fault that it's not done. I work harder than anybody else around here!" The usual outcome of one of these situations is not very productive.

The work is not accomplished. And the persons who were involved have negative feelings about what has happened.

What may be happening in this kind of situation is that each of the participants are operating from ego states which set up specific kinds of ego-state responses within the other. And operating from dissimilar positions discourages any real progress in terms of communication. The boss's original statement is a "parent" kind of statement. Perhaps this forces the employee into his "child" ego state so that from then on there is an impetuous child being chastised by a judgmental parent. If any real progress is to be made, both persons need to get into an adult mode so that they can objectively evaluate the work that needs to be accomplished. The TA approach suggests the use of an analysis of these complex transactions via the parent-adult-child framework to help understand and improve interactions.

Wherever there are unfruitful relationships, one or both parties can explore the problems via TA. TA is useful in the family and in other personal affairs. Do parents relate to each other in an unbiased way? Or do they have patterns of slipping into specific sets of dissimilar ego states: for example, the husband as parent and the wife as child. Do parents allow children to exercise their parent modes?

But the most interesting potential application of TA is within our job environments. Here, like no other place, the problems of hierarchy and authority relationships hinder the clarity of communications. Dr. Rex Hunt has published an article entitled "TA for Managers" in *Management World* in which he suggests the potential power of TA as a tool for executive training, appraisal, and management development. Hunt feels that TA can lead to great improvements at work if persons[3]

1. Select, teach, and use a motivational terminology such as TA with your staff

2. Identify the kind of executive that you wish to be and practice being that way

3. See yourself as a supportive teacher/manager

4. Demonstrate a growth and change attitude
5. Learn to tune into and relate to different ego states
6. Learn to enjoy dealing with child roles
7. Use positive strokes wherever possible
8. Personalize your approach by being yourself
9. Be both firm and fair
    10. Give and ask for personal commitments from your staff

TA shows great promise for stress reduction at work. Careful understanding and use of the framework should assist people in getting to the roots of the feelings of frustration which surround their interpersonal relationships. And for many of us, an intellectual grasp of the reasons for our problems help us to deal with our feelings of anxiety. Beyond this kind of personal application, systematic programs of TA within organizations would surely make great strides toward the elimination of many of the basic causes of stress.

Exercise Programs

It is becoming increasingly obvious to many psysiologists, that the benefits of being "fit" far exceed the simple operational measurements of muscle tone or body strength. The physical, mental, and emotional composition of a person are clearly interconnected in a kind of supercomplex metasystem which has continued to defy definition. But the evidence of the interrelationships is so apparent and so universal that hardly any contemporary researcher would deny the certainty of these interrelationships. Studies have shown, for example, that perfectly healthy persons who have been forced to lie in bed in a hospital environment soon exhibit the symptoms of illness. Conversely many recovery programs are placing increasing emphasis upon "healthy" kinds of activities — the things that one normally associates with feeling good.

While physiologists and exercise therapists have stressed the importance of conditioning for several years now, the results of the research which has recently begun to attach itself to this work shows benefits and involvements which surpass the purely physiological changes in research subjects.

Ismail and Trachtman, physiologists from Purdue, have reported the results of their work with middle-aged businessmen in a large exercise program. After many hundreds of results which supported their theoretical views of the body and its various responses to the conditioning processes, the researchers' attention was increasingly drawn toward some nonphysical implications of exercise.

At first it was just a subliminal sense that something elusive — something that we could not measure with our stethoscopes, biochemical tests, and pulmonary instruments — was happening in the course of the program. After a while we articulated what at first we only felt: we were fairly sure that our paunch, sedentary, middle-aged academics were undergoing personality change, subtly but definitely. While hypochondriacal complaints were endemic at the start of the program — someone was always reporting at least one pre-heart attack symptom to us — by the time the program ended we were hearing few complaints of any type. The men often seemed to become more open and extroverted. Although many of them had known each other well before the program started, by the time they reached the end of the program, they seemed to be interacting more freely and to be more relaxed. Their whole demeanor seemed to us to be more even, stable, and self-confident.[4]

Moving from the original observation, the researchers quickly attempted to measure the impact of exercise upon the mental or emotional "set" of the individual. Using the "Cattell Personality Factor Test," the researchers measured their subjects both before and after a vigorous exercise program. In an effort to sort out the various effects of fitness upon personality factors, Ismail and Trachtman pre-sorted the subjects into two groups: one group which was relatively fit and a second which was not.

Preliminary analysis of the data suggested some differences between these groups even before the program began. The more-fit group scored significantly higher on both emotional stability and imagination. But after the exercise program had ended the less-fit group had not only raised their scores on both of these dimensions to approximately that of the "fit" group, but they also made significant gains on self-sufficiency and the reduction of proneness to guilt.

The general conclusion of their study was that a higher level of physical fitness was associated with emotional maturity, calmness, the ability to accurately perceive reality while being emotionally involved, restraint in avoiding difficulty, an active imagination, enthusiasm, an unconventional or idealistic approach to things, a tendency to become absorbed in ideas, a tendency toward accident proneness, and a very slight predisposition to guilt.

While many of these factors are quite questionable in terms of their impact upon the individual, several would clearly appear to be linked to the kinds of positive results that have been associated with the resolution of stress. Increased calmness, clarity, and imaginative power, for example, have all been positively connected to lower levels of stress. Thus, the prior scientific literature on stress and stress reduction would support the notion of many physiologists, that exercise can serve as a stress-relieving device.

While the research in this particular area is clearly in its infancy, there is every reason to suspect that there are some strong connections between the physical condition and the level of stress of a person. A number of companies have either begun systematic programs of physical fitness or are strongly encouraging their employees to take advantage of in-plant physical facilities during lunch time or other break periods. One Japanese company that I heard about recently employs a physical director who moves through the plant on a fixed schedule leading the workers in calisthenics. An American manufacturing company has recently begun a running program for its executives. Instead of the traditional "business lunch" with its customary martini, executives are encouraged to run laps on the company track and then to eat later at their jobs.

The results of these and other similar programs are highly interesting. They suggest a positive relationship between exercise and stress and productivity.

The Benson Technique

After several years of investigating TM and the impact of

TM upon stress reduction, Dr. Herbert Benson began a serious attempt to develop another technique which duplicated the results of TM. Benson was encouraged by the power of the TM research but he apparently was impatient with Maharishi's rigid plan for training new meditators and his insistence upon the secrecy of the mantra-distribution technique (which is known only to these teachers of TM). Thus Benson set out to invent a simple technique which would work like TM, could be offered free to large numbers of persons, and could be studied in a laboratory setting.

Benson's approach[5] utilizes four steps which are almost universal within meditation techniques.

    1. Choose a calm quiet environment.

    2. Sit in a comfortable position and in a comfortable chair.

    3. Assume a passive attitude (one should not be concerned with his performance, etc.)

    4. Meditate.

The meditation technique suggested by Benson utilizes a single and universal mantra, the word *one*. Meditators are told to breathe in through the nose, and then to breathe out while silently repeating the word *one*. Benson suggests that his technique be continued for twenty minutes and practiced once or twice a day but not within two hours of a meal.

Benson's research findings indicate that his technique shares many of the same benefits of TM. Preliminary results suggest significant decreases in body metabolism and breath rate as a result of his practice. His official position regarding the comparative value for the two techniques is not clear at this time. While he writes about his own techniques, he continues to cite and utilize the practice of TM and its research results as its major theoretical underpinning.

My own judgment suggests that after many years of studying an ageless technique, the Maharishi is in a much better position to understand the intricacies of the mantra-selection process and the subtleties of the application of individual mantras to each person. Thus I would guess that Benson's (or anyone else's) single mantra might not have the same ultimate value as that of a known technique. Thus I would think that if one were to commit several minutes per day to some kind of meditative pursuit he might ultimately benefit from the selection of a "tried" technique. Here again the results of the research would be in favor of TM rather than another approach.

Biofeedback Training

Quite a lot of attention, of late, has been focused upon the study of brain-wave patterns. It has been found that certain brain-wave (electrical) patterns are found to relate to specific types of mental process. Tension or worry is usually accompanied by a particular pattern called *Beta*. Daydreaming is usually associated with a second and different kind of brain pattern called *Theta*. And another, very different brain-wave pattern, known as *Alpha*, is related to relaxation and/or tension reduction.

While science has known of the existence and meaning of these different brain-wave patterns for many years, there has recently been a new interest in the utilization of Alpha-wave monitors for therapeutic work. It has been reasoned that since Alpha is strongly associated with relaxation and/or the reduction of tension, all one needs to do to induce a high level of rest and relaxation is to turn on an Alpha-wave monitor and then learn what he must do to relax. The subject can try different kinds of relaxation techniques, aiming for the particular one or ones which elicit the most success in terms of Alpha-wave production.

The Alpha-wave monitor itself is not a particularly expensive piece of equipment. In fact, the January 1973 *Popular Mechanics* included a simple do-it-yourself model which could be operated on a simple nine-volt battery. Acting as a kind of amplifier, the brain-wave monitor is used in the following way. The subject is connected to a monitor and told to relax in some particular way. When he begins to clear his mind of its clatter and to relax, the Alpha production which follows produces a particular pattern of sounds within the monitor.

The subject, through practice, can learn what things facilitate or discourage the production of Alpha.

The preliminary results of biofeedback training are very exciting, at least in terms of the potential which they suggest for the self-control of bodily functions. Researchers at the Menninger Foundation have discovered that patients can be trained to control migraine headaches. At Wisconsin, subjects were trained to control breath rate independently. And in another experiment, cardiac patients were trained to control their own arrhythmia with feedback apparatus.

The potential for the use of biofeedback training is very exciting. If monitors could be produced for a reasonable price (current models sell within the $100-$400 range), then persons could increasingly gain access to this kind of learning experience. More and more people could have the opportunity to learn how to increase Alpha, thus expanding their ability to relax and to be creative.

Yoga

Perhaps one of the most powerful, but least understood, methods of stress reduction is the practice of yoga. Like TM, yoga is a kind of strange-sounding thing which evokes all kinds of illusions of Indian culture and mysticism. And like TM, the practicing of yoga is actually a very simple, clearcut mechanism which is not really bound to a particular culture or religion. Unlike TM, however, yoga is neither simple nor Americanized in its approach. In fact, the efficient practice of yoga requires both a disciplined mind and body.

At the surface level, the purpose of yoga is to reduce stress or, more particularly, to induce the integrated relaxation of both mind and body. Obviously, however, the ultimate ramifications of yoga are much deeper than that. They include the development of the "whole person" and also the ultimate union with God or "Samadhi," the exalted level of consciousness where the individual merges with the universe.

The mechanics of yoga are fairly simple. Although teaching techniques vary greatly and the emphasis throughout the learning of yoga is upon the personal level of experience, there are three stages within the practice:

1. Hatha yoga — the learning of several physical positions which are oriented toward disciplining the body and then the whole person. This aspect of yoga is perhaps the most apparent to many of us — the lotus, the headstand, and all the other incredibly difficult looking postures which are oriented toward toning and flexibilizing the body. But this is simply one aspect of yoga, an aspect which paves the way for the second step.

2. Pranayana — the systemizing and revitalizing of the breathing mechanism. Essentially this aspect of yoga fixes the attention upon breathing and breath control. Again, the purpose is for the subsequent step.

3. Meditation — the final and most important step in which the person learns to quiet himself and tune his body into the forces of creation.

There are a number of different approaches to yoga meditation. Most are similar to TM in terms of their approach to the process of human development. Many use a mantra or "seed sound" to help the student to learn to become inner-directed.

While there is no substantial body of scientific literature surrounding the practice of yoga and its relationship to such things as productivity at work, there is every reason to believe that its practice reduces stress. When practiced successfully, proponents of yoga techniques report a great range of benefits, including both mental and physical vigor. If yoga does reduce stress, which it clearly seems to do, then it would follow that the practice would be very beneficial for persons who work in superstressed environments and would logically then result in improved productivity.

There are obviously some very deep connections between yoga and TM. For those who are interested in pursuing this relationship, I would suggest a very illuminating and clear work entitled *Autobiography of a Yogi,* by Pramahansa Yogananda.[6]

Prayer

The potential impact of prayer upon the aggregate level of anxiety of an individual is a kind of fundamental truism which most of us have probably held at arm's length while broaching more pragmatic subjects, such as productivity or psychological growth. But surely each of us has had the experience of feeling a kind of "religious" high on a Sunday which is soon lost in the everyday shuffle. In fact, the sheer mention of the word *prayer*, or *church*, or *religion* has usually brought jeers or skepticism from the practical arena of life. It has often bewildered me that the same men who devoutly bow their heads in prayer on Sunday morning would be the first to chuckle if someone at work who was in the midst of a technical problem or an important meeting were to suggest a prayer.

What is this strange and mystical construct, prayer? And why does it play such a mixed part in our lives? What is the impact of prayer and/or religious experience upon the individual? How does it affect our everyday lives?

Theologians are quick to point out that the worship of God (in one form or another) is a universal phenomenon. From the oldest dated cultures or the most removed civilizations, there are continued and universal references to the practice of religion. But until the past few years there had never been much of an attempt to rectify the religious experience with science or the scientific method. The priest, the minister, and the rabbi all stated that prayer was necessary, that prayer was good, that we needed prayer to be healthy and happy.

A few years ago, the Reverend Franklin Loehm[7] opened a proverbial "can of scientific worms." by the publication of an incredible little paperback called *The Power of Prayer on Plants*. In this book, Loehm attempts to verify the impact of prayer scientifically by using an experimental and a control group of plants. In a number of different experiments, he statistically verified the impact of prayer on plant growth. Experimenters used random procedures to sort seeds into two groups. Then using a "standard" prayer and a standardized operational approach to the praying process, the experimental plants were prayed for while the control group was simply handled in the normal way. From that point on, the two groups of plants were handled in an identical fashion in terms of planting, fertilizing, weeding, and sun exposure.

The amazing results of this study were that the plants which had been prayed for were measured to be significantly healthier and larger than the other group of plants.

It is very hard to explain this result in scientific language. And that is due, at least in part, to the inability of scientific language to handle these kinds of phenomena. One thing is very clear, however, and that is the scientifically verifiable power of prayer. It would seem from these findings as well as the many well-publicized cases of miracles or faith-healers, that prayer, taken in a broad context, can have some very substantial effects upon the individual.

A few companies, of late, have experimented with the integration of religious experiences into the work situation. The particular firms which are involved would appear to be small in size and centralized in terms of their control. Perhaps these factors have something to do with the potential of programs for religious involvement.

One plant which I recently investigated has a daily "visiting clergy" program, which consists of both a worship service and a homily by a guest clergy. Different denominations are invited to participate from day to day, and employees are encouraged to attend the daily midmorning services on a voluntary basis.

While my instincts tell me that it will be many years before a substantial number of large companies begin programs like this one, there is every indication that many of the organizational cobwebs which impede this same progress cause much of the stress which we are trying to deal with.

Other Ways of Reducing or Not Reducing Stress

Naturally the content of this chapter is bound by the

limits of my own experiences. I have tried to capture and present a broad range of approaches which might be utilized to reduce stress. There are a few important reasons for the inclusion of this kind of chapter within the book. First it was stated earlier that the purpose here was to explore the nature of and consequences of stress at work rather than the usefulness of a single technique such as TM. So while I continue to feel that TM represents the most powerful and the most efficient available approach to stress reduction, it is impossible to discount the existence and/or the potential of other techniques.

Due to the limitations of my own experience with other stress-oriented techniques I feel compelled to add that there are countless thousands of approaches which have not been included within this volume. They run the gamut from quasi-religious or religious techniques to salesmanship and philosophy to karate. No one could write a complete volume of stress-reduction techniques since the existence and resolution of aggregate stress is such a highly individual matter.

I am sure, for example, that I have not done justice to the power of religious experience in dealing with stress. The Christian experience of confession, the common but little-known practice of faith healing, and other aspects of all of the great religions of the world point the way toward a new understanding of stress resolution. Perhaps the only problem with organized worship is that most of us are too highly stressed to be able to understand or appreciate it!

My experiences lecturing on the subject of stress to practicing managers convince me that there are a few common misconceptions about things which reduce stress. Invariably someone will stand up (shakily) at the end of the typical dinner-speech (with accompanying happy hour and after-dinner cocktail) and say: "I don't need a stress-reducing technique because I always relax with a few martinis after work!" After the typical rounds of boisterous laughter which I take to suggest that a least a few others have begun the same practice, the questioner sits back in his seat with a kind of smug expression and I begin my stock reply. "There is plenty of evidence to suggest that alcohol *causes* rather than reduces stress. And that everyone of us would be doing the most sensible thing possible if he were to stop or at least limit his intake of alcohol." Somehow that comment is analogous to throwing a hand grenade into such a dinner meeting. The typical result is utter silence followed by a barrage of difficult-to-answer questions.

The universality of this experience leads me to believe that many, many people have fallen into the fallacy of thinking that drinking can relax one and reduce his stress. But most of the recent research about drinking suggests a different picture. The use of alcohol probably causes an immediate but short-lived high, which is followed by a disproportionately low low which lasts for a longer time. The final impact upon the "serious" drinker is a kind of vicious-circle effect where the person sinks deeper and deeper into the depths of stress.

A second question which arises often enough to be worthy of mention is the impact of the use of drugs upon stress. Many are deluded into the notion that drugs can reduce stress. Research in this area suggests that drugs are extremely dys-functional in terms of the body's natural mechanisms. It would seem that with very few exceptions the use of prescription or nonprescription drugs discourages the process of stress reduc-tion. So at the risk of being somewhat at odds with a great many current practitioners within the health-care industry, I would suggest that the fewer drugs one takes, the greater one's long-run chances for reducing stress and for using fully the creative capacities which follow. I recently attended a very informative lecture by a young physician from Boston's V.A. Hospital, Dr. David Doner.[8] His position affirms my own. He emphasizes the fact that the human body is a wonderfully efficient, but delicate, organism. And that while it has the complete capacity to continue in optimum health or to cure itself of damage, medical practice many times interferes with that capacity. He was openly critical of the drug-happy culture which we seem to have evolved. When we have trouble sleep-ing we use a sleeping pill; or trouble with feeling sleepy, a stimulant! Nervous? Try one of these tranquilizers! Have a headache or menstrual tension? Use this — no prescription necessary! But what are the full range of effects of these pills that we use? Might they not attack and upset the delicate balance within our bodies? Dr. Doner and many of his colleagues in the medical profession suggest that many of our popular remedies cure one problem but cause another, perhaps more serious, one.

Stress reduction does not usually come from the careful or systematic use of drugs. In fact it is unlikely that the use of drugs could be viewed as even a neutral factor. Persons who are interested in evolving a less anxious, more peaceful, and productive approach to life must learn to fly on their own — to develop natural processes for stress reduction.

The Choice of a Technique: A Comparison

The research here has not attempted to view the difference between stress-reducing techniques. In fact, that kind of research is sorely lacking in the literature. Perhaps this is due to the newness of the entire field of study. Perhaps it is also due to the incredible complexity which would be involved in the cross-evaluation of different approaches.

But in any event it would seem a safe bet, if not a classic understatement, to propose that the stresses which we are all undergoing are not doing us a bit of good. And beyond that simple assertion, the thinking individual might just about be ready to embark upon a systematic program for the reduction of his own stress. What should he do? How does he go about the major job of combating the constant bombardment of stressors from his environment?

The first step must be an intellectual commitment. I want to improve my capacity to deal with life! I want to become a more useful and productive person, to do a better job at home, and a better job at work. I want to be happier and healthier — and the answer to these desires is to recognize and deal with stress rather than to bury my head in the sand and ignore the entire issue.

Having come this far along let me suggest two potential criteria for approaching the problem.

Use a technique that is acceptable
and exciting to you.

How many people including myself have zealously begun programs which they soon forget about. The diets, the anti-smoking therapy, the vow to get into shape once and for all — these are among the classic abandoned plans. I think that the primary requirement for success, beyond the beginning motivation to improve, is a high degree of comfortability with the program. If you absolutely hate all forms of exercise and you have a long history of rejecting your physical fitness perhaps an "exercise to reduce stress" program would be doomed from the start. So I believe that we should all seek programs, or combinations of programs, which are exciting and positive experiences.

Even though my own research suggests that TM is the most efficient technique currently available, I am reluctant to foist this knowledge upon others since I am aware of the fact that many could not or would not be able to accept a concept such as meditation. It is far better to employ a less effective approach consistently than to begin a highly efficient technique, only to give up later.

Use a technique which continues to
be scientifically verifiable.

Scientists are increasingly turning their attention to the question of human potential. And the same ugly reality remains a part of this overall investigation. Mankind continues to operate on substantially less than all eight cylinders. Each of us uses just a small portion of our creative capacity. We might logically expect that the intensity of this kind of stress research will increase. Thus each of use would be wise to turn an eager ear to the results of research in this arena. We might search for and attempt to utilize the most effective techniques (in terms of results) which are available.

chapter 9

Management Prescriptions for the Year 2000

We have come quite a long way in terms of the material presented, since the beginnings of this book. We began with a revealing glimpse of man at work; his problems, his aspirations, and his needs. In Chapter 1, we moved to a discussion of management (perhaps mismanagement would be a better phrase). Chapter 2 attempted to present a simplified approach to sensible management practice. The fact remains, however, that very few managers have been exposed to any kind of formal, sophisticated management training. And this sets the stage for one of the primary sources of stress, the failure of organizational structures. to adapt to the needs of the employees. Chapter 3 detailed some of the major sources of stress and attempted particularly to relate stress to the work environment.

The next few chapters addressed themselves to the discussion and definition of stress as well as the impact of stress upon the person. It was shown that while stress is a serious detriment to the overall quality of life, it is also possible to reduce stress and also to insulate oneself from the effects of a stressful environment. Chapters 6 and 7 attempted to explore the impact of stress upon work performance. Research was presented which supported the notion that reduced stress resulted in great gains in productivity, a fact that could have some very positive results in terms of our own job performance.

The last chapter was included in order to explore the potential value of several methods for stress reduction. It offered alternatives to the original notion of meditation for stress reduction.

So in a very real sense, the book is complete at this point. I have tried to show the difficult position of the employee (at all levels of the organization), the potential for productivity which lies untapped, and a method (TM) for addressing the problem. But I still feel that there is another important job to be done here within these last few pages. I would like to suggest how the typical employee can assimilate this information, and then utilize it within his own job environment. And also what we might expect to happen to the job environment itself.

Change and More Change

If there were one solid prediction which could be made for the year 2000, it would be the continued increase of change. And this is not simply to say that change will continue to exist, but that the rate of change itself will accelerate. Just as the past few decades have witnessed spectacular transitions in production methods, processes, products, new industries, and great educational progress, the next few decades can be expected to provide more and more change. So if we think that we have already been forced to adapt to some rapidly changing conditions, we haven't even gotten a glimpse of what is yet to come.

Bennis[1] has suggested that many of our most difficult problems in dealing with change, both technical and social, are related to the fact that the rate of change, and consequently the rate at which we must adapt to change, is a geometric progression. Figure 9.1 shows the phenomenon in a descriptive way, viewing time on the *x*-axis and the rate of change on the *y*-axis. The slope of the adaptation-rate line begins with a relatively gentle slope but, by the time that it reaches the decade from 1990 to 2000, the change in the rate of change is moving more in ten years than it had changed in the forty years previous. What might happen in the year 2020 is anyone's guess.

Figure 9.1
The Rate of Change: A Geometric
Function

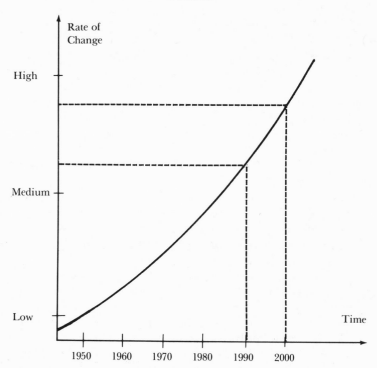

The implications here are almost frightening. Where we used to complain that the production process which we tooled up and carefully engineered would only last for two to three years before it needed a complete rework, the processes of the 2000s may typically last only one year, or perhaps six months. Entire industries may phase in and out of existence faster than production processes used to. Take the plastics industry, for example. There was a time within the immediate recollection of many of us, when that particular industry did not even exist. But those persons who became involved in plastics are probably lulled, just as all of the rest of us in other industries, into the false notion that plastics has always been and always will be. But the historical evidence is to the contrary! Plastics emerged, grew very rapidly, and may now be peaking or even beginning to falter.

While most of the industries which we view as an integral part of the complex industrial environment do not behave as dynamically as plastics, it does not take much more than average hindsight to see that every single one of them behaves in the same fundamental way. An industry moves through a relentless birth-death cycle. Some become so rigidly connected to a single process or a raw material or a product that this cycle is much shorter than others. Others manage to adapt to changes so that while the industry continues, it does so in name only. The generics of some of these changing industries — for example, the computer industry — move so rapidly that the entire business changes except for the name. There have been so many changes in the past twenty years in data processing, for example, that, if a highly competent person could have been instantaneously transported from 1955 to 1975, he would have been completely lost in a foreign environment.

The year 2000 will see many more industries like plastics or black-and-white television which phase in and then out within a working lifetime. And even the most stable industries will be typified by increasing change.

Perhaps the only aspect of 2000 which will remain relatively unchanged will be the person. He will be unchanged in terms of his definition as an organizational component, but changed substantially in terms of his needs to adapt to the change. Few, if any, workers in the next century will find comfortable, predictable, or stable environments in which to work.

A Temporary Society

Borrowing more of the work of Warren Bennis[2] we might look for a very substantial change in both technical and social structures in the year 2000. It will increasingly become obvious that the rigid bureaucratic model of Max Weber upon which the industrial revolution was mounted cannot deal effectively with rapid change.

It might be expected therefore that democratic or participative structure will gradually replace the bureaucratic norm. But this will not happen easily or without its share of major difficulties. We saw earlier that perhaps the major importance of Weber's bureaucracy was that it provided a good deal of stability for both work and social cultures. An industrial environment which was composed of a series of interrelated bureaucracies provided a highly predictable and clear-cut system of careers and rewards for those persons who would take the time to understand and then work toward a visible goal. The gradual transition of bureaucracy towards democratic processes systematically eats away at this stability. No longer is there a "sure-fire" path to success: Get A's in high school, go to college, major in engineering, get a job in a training program, be a good engineer, become the engineering manager, etc. Instead, the exceptions become the rules. Persons who follow acceptable guidelines are not rewarded as their predecessors were. Also, many successful persons turn out to be individuals who have rejected the "normal" career matters. In short, each of us will be left adrift in our own attempt to plot a course by taking a series of guesses about what we should be doing.

Now there is something to be said about this new environment where each of us must be responsible enough to think through the most fundamental decisions regarding career, job, etc. But how many of us are really ready to take over this kind of responsibility? Can we be the masters of our own destiny?

Realistically speaking, we will have to become willing and able to make our own decisions about jobs and careers. The forces of change will make temporary organizations the rule rather than the exception. So if the seventies are seen as a period of transition away from bureaucratic process and toward democracy, then the 2000s will be the organization age of democracy. Structures will no longer provide the stable career patterns which they once did. Instead they will evolve in response to a need and then dissipate. The dominant social structure might begin to look more like a construction-job site with its coordinated teams of tradesmen, than like a personnel chart for IBM or General Motors.

We can also expect that the emphasis in human organization will increasingly move from manufacturing or production in orientation to other service kinds of perspectives. The United States has long since passed the magic point where its productive energies have begun to lean more toward service and less toward manufacturing. That means that, as time goes on, more and more of us find ourselves working in people- or service-oriented work rather than at a manufacturing facility. This places still another strain upon the process of democratization since the people-related industries face a much more dynamic and changeable kind of task, in general, than the product-orientated production industries.

The year 2000 will be accompanied by temporary organizations.[3] People will come together in organized networks of groups to solve dynamic problems, and as these problems are solved, the organizations which produced the solutions will cease to exist.

The Outlook for Management Practice

The burden of the twenty-first century will be placed upon the administrative function. It will be the task of managers to coordinate the contributions of individual professionals who work within temporary adaptive organizations trying to accomplish complex patterns of dynamic goals. Surely this will be a monumental task! But can the theory and the practice of management change rapidly enough to prepare for the year 2000?

Ten years ago, forward-thinking management theorists might have answered that question with an emphatic no! But since the systems-theory influence in management and the new emphasis upon the sophisticated empirical work such as the contingency-theory research of Lawrence and Lorsch,[4] that answer might be changing. Management has made some dramatic steps in terms of behavioral, quantitative, and research sophistication in the past few years, so much so that the quality of journals in the field has skyrocketed within this past decade. But obviously this theoretical and research competence, by itself, is not adequate for creating change in the work environments of the bulk of the work force. The trick is to move the growing mass of sophisticated management theory from the books and journals of academia into the hands of the practical people who need it.

What we are faced with during this transition period between the industrial age and the postindustrial society is an incredible need for management education. Almost all of us are in dire need of the interpersonal skills that must accompany democratic organization. The process of change has been so swift and so punctuated by short-term success that leaders and participants will have to be educated in the theory and practice of management. The major underlying problem with management reduction is that the relatively rapid transition from the industrial revolution, through a highly industrialized society, and finally toward the postindustrial era, has demanded corollary changes in management practice. The typical assembly-line or punch-press work of the turn of the century lent itself quite readily to the bureaucratic form of organization. Thus, persons who were involved in that kind of work were continually reinforced by their own efforts to increase the level of autocracy where they worked. They "learned" from their success and helped to foster an entire autocratic or theory-X[5] ethic for management.

The new problem arises from the fact that before this "X"

ethic could completely dissolve itself, the need for a very different approach has emerged. And due to the long record of the relatively successful use of an autocratic model at work, it is hard for most of us to adopt the opposite approach.

Perhaps the greatest problem for management practice is not the industrial revolution era or the opposite postindustrial society. Perhaps the major hassles lie in the transition period where Table 9.1 suggests that mixed modes of behavior, structure, and leadership are required for success. The problems stem from the fact that the transition period contains a combination of simple or repetitive work as well as highly complex work. Thus the practitioner who has no systematic understanding of management theory is left to guess about how he should proceed.

So the question for management practice in the postindustrial era would seem to be this:

Can management education keep pace with both the transitions in twenty-first century work patterns and the increasing sophistication in management research?

I have every reason to believe that this can and will happen. It would seem that the entire field of management is growing dramatically in both size and sophistication. More and more colleges and universities are offering both strong programs in undergraduate management education, and the MBA (Master of Business Administration) degree.

The Management of Change

The process of twenty-first century management will be unlike our contemporary notions of what leadership and administration are all about. Since patterns of work will become highly complex and dynamic, patterns of management will become the same. The obvious implication of this rapidly increasing level of difficulty is that more and more organizational participants will need to become directly involved in the administrative affairs of the organization. Each employee will have to become more of a decision-maker, a planner, and an organizer of work for both himself and his colleagues. Natu-

Table 9.1
Postindustrial Society:
The Implications of the Transition

Characteristic	Time Frame		
	1900	1950	2000
Description of the era	Industrial Revolution	Industrial Age	Postindustrial Society
Dominant kind of task	Simple and repetitive	Mixture of simple and complex	Very complex
Type of organizational structure required	Autocratic	Mixed	Democratic
Predominant management error	Not autocratic enough	Mixed	Too autocratic
Skills required by organizational participants	Ability to accept autocratic structure and follow orders	Mixed	Self-starter No need for authority
Leadership modes required for success	Theory X or military approach	Mixed	Participative or democratic

rally this will make the coordination of efforts within organizations a major difficulty and place more and more of a burden upon administrations. Our traditional notion of a "manager" might well be replaced by the "managerial function" which will be shared by all of the participants of modern organizations.

With so many persons becoming directly involved in the process of administrating their own work, the rate of change in both technical and social structures at work is bound to increase dramatically. Thus the management of the twenty-first century will focus upon change. And the key question of this change management might be as follows:

> How can participants in organizations accept and deal with rapid and never-ending change in their working environments even though the very existence of this change is uncomfortable and stress producing for all of us?

There have been many attempts at understanding or dealing with resistance to change. Most of these have been unsuccessful. And perhaps this is due to the simple fact that high levels of change lead to high levels of stress which lead to anxiety, tension, nervousness, antisocial behavior, and a number of other reactions which might be lumped into the syndrome which has been identified as "resistance to change." Perhaps the fact that people resist change is because they must.

The management of change, that is to say, the management of the postindustrial age, requires *the management of stress*.

Predictions for the Year 2000 and Beyond

Perhaps the best way to lay the foundation for stress management is to begin a general discussion of the kinds of changes which will be evidenced by the next century. We have already seen that the key notion for dealing with patterns of work in the twenty-first century is the recognition and the acceptance of the process of change itself. But a more successful framework for dealing with change (and also with stress) might be based upon an understanding of the kinds of transitions which are the most likely to occur.

The purpose of this section, then, is not to project broad-based socioeconomic or political changes. It would seem quite obvious that these kinds of issues are connected to the notion of work behavior, but for purposes of brevity and practicality we will limit the discussion to the kinds of changes which affect the primary work organization itself.

While any kind of projection into the future must admittedly incorporate some kind of guesswork, the following predictions are presented on the basis of mounting evidence. In addition, each of these concepts represents a substantial departure from most of the existing notions that we have accepted about the world of work.

Attitudes toward Work

The first major difference that will emerge within the next century involves the basic attitude of people toward their work. Twentieth-century man has, to a large extent, been caught up in a work ethic within which he has defined not only his success but his identity in terms of his work. Twenty-first-century man will avoid this dilemma. The Protestant work ethic will die. And it will become not only possible, but very acceptable, to be unemployed. It will be feasible through the use of government and other special programs, as well as the benevolence of friends and family, for a person to exist with a bare minimum of effort expended toward gainful employment. Perhaps a part-time job now and then to purchase a large or a luxury item will be all that is required to make a reasonably acceptable living.[6]

The major impact of this change will not be felt in the size or the lifestyle of the welfare society. While it is undoubtedly true that a larger number of people will choose to "drop out" either for a short time (until they reorient themselves), or permanently, the greatest changes will take place at work. Since companies will have lost their "necessities of life" hammerlock on employees, they will be increasingly forced to offer attractive and purposeful alternatives to leisure time. Jobs will need to become responsible and rewarding experiences by organizational design rather than by accident. The kinds of work assignments which are universally regarded as difficult or boring will be either be designed away or automated, regardless of the cost.

This new attitude toward work will certainly affect the career decisions of workers. There will be an increasing orientation toward doing what is fun or rewarding or useful rather than simply doing the thing that can earn a person the most money and social status.

Workers and organizations will be motivated to develop a new honesty in dealing with each other. There will be little or no reason to withhold information either for fear of reprisal or because we are concerned about ruining our careers.

Naturally this will place an increased burden upon the administration of an organization and more particularly upon the managers who will need to design twenty-first-century jobs for twenty-first-century workers.

Demographics

The Zero Population Growth[7] emphasis of the later sixties has certainly demonstrated a most fundamentally incorrect supposition that was part of the American culture for many years: The Growth Ethic. We have grown to accept ever-increasing population and growth rates as a part of reality. This has led to, among other things, the popularly accepted notion that "growth" is an ideal. Most companies in the 1950s, for example, held "growth" to be one of their major goals.

The twenty-first century may witness a radical departure from the growth ethic. Companies will begin to orient themselves toward an objective evaluation of demographic characteristics. Stability or even size reduction may become just as important in light of other organizational goals, as growth once was.

This new approach will have broad sweeping implications for marketing, personnel, and other aspects of twenty-first-century business.

Human-Resources Management

Competition for employees as well as the new attitudes toward work will probably bring about a greatly increased emphasis upon "human-resources management." Organizations will expand their personnel functions to include some very systematic approaches toward analyzing and fitting employees to the optimum places within organizations.[8]

The first emphasis will probably be to draw upon behavioral sophistication and, more particularly, psychological testing to more thoroughly understand the needs and aspirations of employees at all levels. Attitudes, leadership styles, followership needs, occupational preference testing, and other such individual criteria may be collected and analyzed in an attempt to fit people in the best possible jobs. It is very probable that this kind of information will be fed into computer programs, which might use linear-programming techniques to deploy employees throughout an organization in a way that minimizes both organizational and individual conflicts!

This new orientation toward the value and impact of participants in organizations will probably cause a major change in other areas of organizational functioning. Accounting practice, for example, might expand to include the kind of human-asset accounting that was suggested by Rensis Likert[9] many years ago. The values of individual employees, in terms of training, experience, competence, and importance to the business, might be entered in the operating books and the balance sheets of organizations. In this way, reasonably intelligent decisions might be made regarding wage payment, the cost of transfers, or the losses due to turnover.

Organizational Structure

There can be no doubt about the fact that organizational structures will be making radical changes in the direction of participativeness or democracy. And there will be two equally strong motives for this transition.

Democracy will emerge as the only sensible way in which to deal with the complexities of the next century. Technical change, social change, and work change taken together will be just too much for the traditional bureaucratic model to cope with. Naturally, there will be vestiges of the past in even the most sophisticated organization, such as the "old-fashioned manager" who graduated from college way back in 1965 when they were teaching better ways to do industrial engineering. But the primary emphasis will be in the area of participative management.

Democracy will also emerge as the only feasible way to cope effectively with large numbers of highly motivated professional persons. And it will soon be evident that these competent employees of the twenty-first century who choose to work for one or more reasons will not accept the impersonal theme of autocratic management practice.

Patterns of Work

Just as surely as we might expect some rather severe changes in attitudes toward work, organizational structure, and human-resources management, we can expect some relatively large-scale changes in approaches to work itself. In fact, these changes in work hours and days have already begun to take place in many firms.

Perhaps the most apparent reason for expecting these kinds of changes stems from the fact that there is no sensible reason for the kinds of work patterns which we have evolved. Why, for example, do so many of us begin work exactly at 8:00 A.M.? Or why do we work five days per week? What is the magic surrounding forty hours per week? The fact remains that these standards have emerged on the basis of long standing traditions and that further changes in the evolution of work patterns might be expected to focus upon the flexibility of work patterns rather than arriving at newer or more liberal policies.

The first obvious change will be in the direction of the flexible workweek. Riva Poor[10] has pioneered the research in this area in her popular paperback, *Four Days, Forty Hours.* Most of the studies cited by Poor reflect the great benefits which have been reaped by organizations which have moved to new arrangements of their workdays. The theme within this approach to work improvement is that there is no logical relationship between the kind of work which is being done by a particular organization, and the typical five-day Monday-through-Friday approach. In many cases, some great benefits can be forthcoming by the staggering or overlapping of shifts. A large metropolitan police force, cited by Poor, noticed that the incidence of crime had a peak time and some corresponding low periods. Late-night and early-evening crimes far outweighed afternoon or morning crime, But with a typical five-day, three-shifts-per-day approach, police could not easily be increased at peak crime times. The answer to this problem was to shorten the number of workdays per week per policeman and then to overlap the elongated shifts at high crime times. The result was to double the intensity of police coverage at peak times.

In still another of Poor's examples, a retail outlet advertised itself as the "The Four-Day Tire Company," and opened only Thursday through Sunday. The result was that employees enjoyed continuing three-day weekends, customers could be insured of expanded hours on the four days of business, and the company saved a good deal of overhead.

Riva Poor's examples go on and on. They suggest that a fresh look at shift lengths and times can almost always provide an advantage to the firm. In addition, employees usually find that the four-day or three-and-a-half-day (or whatever) workweek provides a very useful vehicle for improving the quality of their personal lives. There are more and larger blocks of vacation or personal time. And in addition, employees find that Monday-Tuesday-Wednesday weekends are not nearly as crowded as traditional Saturday-Sunday weekends.

The second, and interrelated, change which is being experimented with by a large number of firms is the flexible workday. Instead of being told to work from 9:00 A.M. to 4:30 P.M., employees are given a time range within which they must work a given number of hours. Perhaps they are asked to work for eight hours between the hours of 6:00 A.M. and 8:00 P.M. Or perhaps they are simply asked to work for forty hours between Monday at 6:00 A.M. and Friday at 6:00 P.M.

Most of the objections that could reasonably be leveled at either flexible workweeks or work hours would revolve about the problem of maintaining an assembly line or more simply the continuity in the flow of products through a process. And surely there is every reason to suspect that the more an organization approaches an assembly-line approach, the more difficult the application of flexible work strategies, Perhaps the flexible workweek is much more applicable here than the flexible-work-hours concept itself.

It is important to note, however, that the twenty-first century will be much less assembly-line-oriented than the twentieth-century work world. Thus we might expect to see more and more applications for flexible work patterns. This approach to work planning holds the tangential benefit of easing peak loads on such things as roads, electric power stations, and other public facilities. Since we will not all be rushing home at 5:00 P.M. or to the tennis courts at 6:30 P.M. then we might be able to do with fewer of these expensive systems. The effect could be a great savings to the worker as taxpayer.

Professionalism

Perhaps the primary emphasis within the next fifty years or so will be upon increasing levels of professionalism. The past few decades have clearly indicated that the process of professionalization is the best path to both economic success and prestige. Those group of workers who have succeeded in developing strong organizations which control such factors as how many persons should enter the profession, what their qualifications need to be, how they will be trained, and what they will do, have achieved the highest levels of success.

In addition to these economically oriented criteria, the very nature of professional groups lends itself better to complex jobs and to temporary, democratic organizations. Thus, persons of the next century should increasingly be motivated to seek professionalism. The work world of the future will most likely consist of a loosely organized cartel of professional people who are only temporarily linked to the organizations in which they work, and then by virtue of their areas of expertise. These professions will make significant strides in the direction of dictating their own job descriptions. For example, the accountant of 1975, to a large extent, does what his company tells him to do at work. The same is true for engineers, purchasing agents, etc. These professions in their present forms offer fairly nonspecific guidelines for practitioners who work at individual companies. The accountant or engineer of the twenty-first century however, will relate to his organization in much the same way as a physician who becomes the "company doctor." First of all, it would be an unusual M.D. who would restrict his medical practice to any one company. More than likely the company doctor is first and foremost a "professional" physician who includes that particular company, for some number of hours per week, as a component of a much larger practice. Perhaps this is the way in which the professionals of the 2000s will operate! Applying their skills to a number of different organizations at any given time.

Those persons who do not manage to fulfill the requirements for specific professions will find themselves tied to organizations in much the same way that most employees are now working. Because of their lack of specific marketable skills they will also find themselves at the bottom economic rung of society.

Women at Work

Recent developments in Women's Rights, taken by themselves, would be enough to suggest that the twenty-first-century work world will be quite different in respect to our current notion of a set of male-dominated organizations. Surely the past few years have opened up a new potential of fulfilling, rewarding, and lucrative careers for women. And beyond the defensiveness and resistance of most men who now hold down the policy-making positions in large organizations, perhaps the reason for this phenomenon lies with women themselves. The fact remains that most women are not too interested in becoming "liberated."

Isaac Asimov,[11] one of the greatest writers of our times, has recently addressed this phenomenon in an article entitled "The Falling Birthrate." Asimov has suggested that the changing birthrate (which was discussed in a previous section of this chapter) will eventually force a dramatic change in both family and work structures.

We have evolved a mother-in-the-family-while-father-works system because past social and cultural pressures caused large families. The large numbers of children in the family forced a division of labor (mother versus father), and provided an equitable volume of work for the wife who was in charge of domestic engineering. But the future, according to Asimov, indicates a set of interrelated pressures upon this traditional system.

First, the United States and other developing countries are very clearly moving toward a significantly reduced birthrate. Within the next century there will be significant social pressure to have two or perhaps fewer children. In fact, it will probably become quite acceptable for married people not to have any children at all. However, underdeveloped countries which account for the greatest proportion of the world's population will continue to increase both their population size and growth rate. Thus the pressure and world resources will continue to mount against the more developed countries. The impact of this in the United States, for example, will be a continuing difficulty in maintaining existing standards of living.

Thus pressures on the woman are going to mount. She will no longer be asked to bear and to rear ten or twelve children. Instead she will be expected to rear one or two children quickly, and then get to work to help support the family. Families who choose to live on only one income could well be forced into a lower-middle-class stratum, regardless of the husband's profession. Since the pressures are going to force her into the work world anyway, then the typical woman is going to seek the most rewarding and useful career possible.

Twenty-first-century working society will see many changes which would seem foreign or even inconceivable to most of us today. Not the least of these changes is that the work force will be almost half female rather than almost all male.

The Successful Management of Stress

In an earlier chapter we found that there were at least two approaches to the complex problem of stress management — an intellectual approach and an emotional approach. One focuses upon understanding the situation, while the other is concerned with making realistic changes in the person's ability to function. Effective stress management requires both!

If one is to deal successfully with an increasingly complex and stressful world such as the work world of 2000 or 2100, he must both understand and deal with his own stress reactions. Clearly, then, the worker of the twenty-first century must begin to recognize both the stress agents within his own working environment and their effect upon him. Having made this kind of an analysis of his situation he must then begin a lifelong attack against stress.

Each of us needs to find and utilize a stress-relieving technique to insulate against and release the aggregate stresses which will be associated with the world where we are going. We might think of this as a kind of space voyage into a place with a poisonous environment and equip ourselves with the necessary stress antitoxins. And surely the actual battle against stress requires more than a simple intellectual awareness of what stress is all about. Simply knowing that there is no oxygen on the moon doesn't protect the astronaut who decides to skip across the moon's atmosphere without his oxygen helmet! Likewise the stress fighter is only doing half the job if he simply knows about stress. His choices are to either stay in a locked room for the rest of his life (which could potentially be very stressful) or to seek a stress-reducing technique so that he can safely "skip across the surface of the moon with everyone else." Perhaps the most important single decision which each of us must make is to select a program of stress maintenance.

The next and final important question here concerns the sphere of application for stress management. Is stress management an individual strategy or is it primarily a managerial tool?

The answer, of course, is that stress management should be used at both the individual and the organizational level. Like most other programs of development it is at least hard and perhaps impossible to prescribe something for everyone else and not do it yourself. Many executives or middle managers have attempted to execute large-scale programs of human relations or MBO, only to fail miserably because they didn't apply the technique to themselves first. I, personally, do not think that it is possible to get anyone to improve in terms of a skill that you ignore yourself.

Thus, my own conclusion regarding stress-management applications is that each person must begin by detoxifying or (if you prefer) unstressing himself. Once this procedure is well under way, that person may proceed with a larger application; in other words he may begin to apply stress management to his colleagues at work.

Epilogue

As I conclude this book I feel I must make some comments about the total impact of the work which has been presented. To say that I am personally excited about this book would be a gross understatement of my feelings. Beyond the pride which one must feel having organized and executed such a volume, I feel that this particular book is potentially of great benefit to almost everyone who holds a job. It took me several years of hammering away at this nebulous problem of job satisfaction to begin to understand what was causing the bulk of the problems with people at work. And even then I spent many years lost in the mire of interconnected theories.

I have now come to the fundamental belief that stress is the major factor that reduces the happiness as well as the productivity of workers at all levels of organizations. I further believe that no simple management theory or intellectualization, taken by itself, can solve the problems of work and work-stress. Instead each worker must combat the problem of stress in his own way. He must recognize the existence and impact of stress, and then deal with that stress by employing a stress-reducing technique. It is further apparent to me that TM is very rapidly emerging as the most simple, easy-to-learn, and powerful stress-reducing technique.

Beyond the research evidence presented here, I have seen the giant benefits which have been associated with the application of TM for stress reduction. I have personally experienced some very positive effects based upon my own experiences with TM. I have seen great changes in colleagues who have begun the technique. And, finally, I have watched incredible improvements within a number of organizations which have encouraged the use of TM among their employees.

I feel that everyone needs to utilize some kind of technique for coping with work-oriented stress. He might choose an exercise program, yoga, or some other method rather than TM, but it is critical that he begin some kind of program for coping with his stresses.

I hope that everyone who reads this book will join me in a continuing effort to increase the quality of his or her life by recognizing and dealing with stress!

Appendix

Leadership Style

The purpose of this instrument is to measure leadership style or the natural approaches which you choose to take in dealing with other people. The questions which follow are designed to help you learn about yourself so please try to answer them as honestly as you can.

Work rapidly and complete all of the twenty items if possible. If there is a particular item which you don't understand or you can't answer, simply skip it.

After you have completed the items below, instructions for scoring and interpreting the results will follow.

Read each of the twenty statements, determine if you strongly agree, agree, have mixed feelings, disagree, or strongly disagree: Then place a check mark in the appropriate position.

	Strongly Agree	Agree	Mixed Feelings	Disagree	Strongly Disagree
1. When I tell a subordinate to do something I expect him to do it with no questions asked. After all, I am responsible for what he will do, not him.	(1)	(2)	(3)	(4)	(5)

	Strongly Agree	Agree	Mixed Feelings	Disagree	Strongly Disagree
2. Tight control by a leader usually does more harm than good. People will generally do the best job when they are allowed to exercise self-control.	(5)	(4)	(3)	(2)	(1)
3. Although discipline is important in an organization, the effective leader should mediate his use of disciplinary procedures with his knowledge of the people and the situation.	(1)	(2)	(3)	(4)	(5)
4. A leader must make every effort to subdivide the tasks of his people to the greatest extent possible.	(1)	(2)	(3)	(4)	(5)
5. Shared leadership or truly democratic process in a group can only work when there is a recognized leader who assists the process.	(1)	(2)	(3)	(4)	(5)
6. As leader I am ultimately responsible for all of the actions of my group. If our activities result in benefits for the organization, I should be rewarded accordingly.	(1)	(2)	(3)	(4)	(5)
7. Most persons require only minimum direction on the part of their leader in order to do a good job.	(5)	(4)	(3)	(2)	(1)
8. One's subordinates usually require the control of a strict leader.	(1)	(2)	(3)	(4)	(5)

	Strongly Agree	Agree	Mixed Feelings	Disagree	Strongly Disagree
9. Leadership might be shared among participants of a group so that at any one time there could be two or more leaders.	(5)	(4)	(3)	(2)	(1)
10. Leadership should generally come from the top, but there are some logical exceptions to this rule.	(5)	(4)	(3)	(2)	(1)
11. The disciplinary function of the leader is simply to seek democratic opinions regarding problems as they arise.	(5)	(4)	(3)	(2)	(1)
12. The engineering problems, the management time, and the worker frustration caused by the division of labor are hardly ever worth the savings. In the typical case, workers could do the best job of determining their own job cycles.	(5)	(4)	(3)	(2)	(1)
13. The leader ought to be the group member whom the others elect to coordinate their activities and to represent the group to the rest of the organization.	(5)	(4)	(3)	(2)	(1)
14. A leader needs to exercise some control over his people.	(1)	(2)	(3)	(4)	(5)
15. There must be one and only one recognized leader in a group.	(1)	(2)	(3)	(4)	(5)

		Strongly Agree	Agree	Mixed Feelings	Disagree	Strongly Disagree
16.	A good leader must establish and strictly enforce an impersonal system of discipline.	___ (1)	___ (2)	___ (3)	___ (4)	___ (5)
17.	Basically, people are responsible for themselves and no one else. Thus a leader can not be blamed for or take credit for the work of his subordinates.	___ (5)	___ (4)	___ (3)	___ (2)	___ (1)
18.	Discipline codes should be flexible and they should allow for individual decisions by the leader given each particular situation.	___ (5)	___ (4)	___ (3)	___ (2)	___ (1)
19.	The job of the leader is to relate to his subordinates the task to be done, to ask them for the ways in which it can best be accomplished, and then to help arrive at a consensus plan of attack.	___ (5)	___ (4)	___ (3)	___ (2)	___ (1)
20.	A position of leadership implies the general superority of its incumbent over his workers.	___ (1)	___ (2)	___ (3)	___ (4)	___ (5)

Now that you have completed the leadership profile you may score your own test by simply adding the numbers in parentheses below your check marks. For example, if you scored item 1, strongly agree, the point value in parentheses is "1." To obtain your leadership style, add all of the answers and then take the average. Unless you skip an item you will be dividing by 20. So if your point total is 64, then your leadership style is 64÷20 or 3.2.

To interpret this score you should consult the next table.

Leadership Score	Meaning	(Manager)
2.1 or less	Very autocratic	No. 1
2.2 to 2.7	Relatively autocratic	No. 2
2.8 to 3.2	Mixed style (Components of both democracy & autocracy)	No. 3
3.3 to 3.8	Relatively democratic	No. 4
3.9 or more	Very democratic	No. 5

Followership Style

The purpose of this instrument is to measure followership style or the natural preferences which you might have for your own boss — how he should relate to you in terms of his leadership style. Since these items are designed to help you to learn about yourself you should make every effort to answer them honestly.

Work rapidly and complete all of the sixteen items if possible. However, if there are a few statements which you feel that you cannot answer, simply skip these and continue through the test.

After you have completed the questionnaire, you will be shown how to grade and interpret your results.

Read each of the sixteen items carefully. Determine whether you strongly agree, agree, have mixed feelings, disagree, or strongly disagree. Place a check mark in the appropriate position.

	Strongly Agree	Agree	Mixed Feelings	Disagree	Strongly Disagree
1. I expect my job to be very explicitly outlined for me.	— (1)	— (2)	— (3)	— (4)	— (5)

	Strongly Agree	Agree	Mixed Feelings	Disagree	Strongly Disagree
2. When the boss says to do something I do it. After all he is the boss.	(1)	(2)	(3)	(4)	(5)
3. Rigid rules and regulations usually cause me to become frustrated and inefficient.	(5)	(4)	(3)	(2)	(1)
4. I am ultimately responsible for and capable of self-discipline based upon my contacts with the people around me.	(5)	(4)	(3)	(2)	(1)
5. My jobs should be made as short in duration as possible so that I can achieve efficiency through repetition.	(1)	(2)	(3)	(4)	(5)
6. Within reasonable limits I will try to accommodate requests from persons who are not my boss since these requests are typically in the best interest of the company anyhow.	(5)	(4)	(3)	(2)	(1)
7. When the boss tells me to do something which is the wrong thing to do it is his fault not mine when I do it.	(1)	(2)	(3)	(4)	(5)
8. It is up to my leader to provide a set of rules by which I can measure my performance.	(1)	(2)	(3)	(4)	(5)
9. The boss is the boss. And the fact that he has been promoted suggests that he has something on the ball.	(1)	(2)	(3)	(4)	(5)

	Strongly Agree	Agree	Mixed Feelings	Disagree	Strongly Disagree
10. I only accept orders from my boss.	(1)	(2)	(3)	(4)	(5)
11. I would prefer for my boss to give me general objectives and guidelines and allow me to do the job my way.	(5)	(4)	(3)	(2)	(1)
12. If I do something which is not right it is my own fault, even if my supervisor told me to do it.	(5)	(4)	(3)	(2)	(1)
13. I prefer jobs which are not repetitious, the kind of task which is new and different each time.	(5)	(4)	(3)	(2)	(1)
14. My supervisor is in no way superior to me by virtue of his position. He simply does a different kind of job, one which includes a lot of managing and co-ordinating.	(5)	(4)	(3)	(2)	(1)
15. I expect my leader to give me disciplinary guidelines.	(1)	(2)	(3)	(4)	(5)
16. I prefer to tell my supervisor what I will or, at least, should be doing. It is I who am ultimately responsible for my own work.	(5)	(4)	(3)	(2)	(1)

To score the followership profile you must add the numbers which appear in parentheses below your check marks. For example, if you scored item 1, strongly agree, the point value in parentheses is "1." To obtain your followership style, add each of the answers and then take the average. Unless you omitted an item you will be dividing by 16. If your point total is 32, for example, your followership style is 32÷16 or 2.0. To interpret the score, please refer to the table below.

Followership Score	Meaning	
2.1 or less	Very autocratic	(No. 1)
2.2 to 2.7	Relatively autocratic	(No. 2)
2.8 to 3.2	Mixed	(No. 3)
3.3 to 3.8	Relatively democratic	(No. 4)
3.9 or more	Very democratic	(No. 5)

Notes

CHAPTER 1

1 References to earlier institutions are abundant within the writings of early management theorists — Henri Fayol, for example, took a good deal of his work from the writings of Napoleon.

2 Max Weber, *Theory of Social and Economic Organization* (Glencoe, Illinois: Free Press, 1947).

3 Frederick Taylor, *Principles of Scientific Management* (New York: Harper, 1911).

4 Henri Fayol, *General and Industrial Management* (London: Pitman & Sons, 1949).

5 F.J. Roethlisberger and W.J. Dickson, *Management and the Worker* (Cambridge, Massachusetts: Harvard Press, 1939).

6 Douglas McGregor, *The Human Side of Enterprise* (New York: McGraw-Hill, 1960).

7 Frederick Hertzberg, *Motivation to Work* (New York: Wiley, 1959).

8 Chris Argyris, *Integrating the Individual and the Organization* (New York: Wiley, 1964).

9 Rensis Likert, *New Patterns of Management* (New York: McGraw Hill, 1961).

10 Warren Bennis, *Changing Organizations* (New York: McGraw-Hill, 1966).

11 Alvin Toffler, *Future Shock* (New York: McGraw-Hill, 1972).

CHAPTER 2

1 Prior to the systematic studies of the late sixties which began to pave

the way toward a science of management, the field might best have been described as a kind of art, rather than a predictable or teachable science.

2 McGregor presented his theory X versus theory Y which served to articulate the dichotomy between sides in the management controversy: classical versus human relations.

3 Paul Lawrence and Jay Lorsch, *Organization and Environment* (New York: Irwin, 1965).

4 Fiedler is perhaps the best-known contemporary leadership theorist. His works are prolific throughout the research literature.

5 For an empirical illustration of this statement see: D.R. Frew and R.J. Volpe, "The Management of Teaching Style." *Improving College and University Teaching Journal*, Summer 1973, p-173.

6 It is so easy to view bad work and simply blame it upon the "employees." That strategy requires no introspection, no change, no effort, plus it neatly avoids the assignment of responsibility to ourselves. The only problem is that that strategy is not fruitful either.

CHAPTER 3

1 This concept has been developed by Edgar Schein, noted organizational psychologist. For more information see: *Organizational Psychology* (Englewood Cliffs, N.J.: Prentice-Hall, 1965).

2 Whyte, Wiliam H. *The Organization Man* (Garden City, N.Y.: Doubleday & Co., 1956).

3 Bennis, Warren, *Changing Organizations* (New York: McGraw-Hill Book Co., 1966).

4 Toffler, Alvin, *Future Shock* (New York: Random House, 1970).

CHAPTER 4

1 Selye is *the* recognized authority in the area of stress. He, in fact, coined the term *stress* as it is applied to the human being. His theory of stress is captured in *The Stress of Life* (New York: McGraw-Hill, 1965).

2 Herbert Benson, "Your Innate Asset for Combating Stress," *Harvard Business Review*, July-Aug. 1974, Vol. 52, p. 49.

3 Hans Selye, *The Stess of Life*, p 54.

4 Each of these diseases has been isolated in terms of its relationship to stress by Selye in *The Stress of Life*. The nature and scope of the experimental work is outlined in chapters 15 through 18.

5 These statistics were taken from a lecture by Dr. Harold Bloomfield at a symposium entitled "Improving Productivity Through Stress Reduction," which was held at Rensselaer Polytechnic Institute in Troy, N.Y., on March 19, 1974.

6 This opinion has been expressed by Dr. Harold Bloomfield and other medical experts.

CHAPTER 5

1 *The Wall Street Journal,* 31 August 1972, p. 1.

2 Robert Wallace, *TM and Cardiac Output,* Ph.D. dissertation (Berkeley: University of California, 1970).

3 A. Kasamatsu and T. Hria, "Science of Fazen" *Journal of Psychiatric Neurology* (Japan), 1966, pp. 86-91).

4 *The New York Times,* 11 December 1972, p. 1.

5 R.K. Wallace, "The Physiological Effects of TM," *Science,* 1970 Vol. 167, pp. 1751-1754.

6 H. Benson, "Yoga for Drug Abuse." *The New England Journal of Medicine,* 1969, Vol. 281, p. 1133.

7 R.K. Wallace, and H. Benson, "The Physiology of Meditation," *Scientific American,* 1972, Vol. 226, No. 2, pp. 84-90.

8 Ibid, p. 8.

9 Ibid.

10 Wallace, Benson, and Wilson, "A Wakeful Hypometabolic, Physiologic State," *American Journal of Physiology,* 1971, Vol. 221, No. 2, pp. 795-799.

11 Honsberger and Wilson, "TM in Treating Asthma," *Respiratory Therapy,* 1973, Vol. 2, No. 2, p 197.

12 J. Allison, "Respiratory Changes During TM," *The Lancet,* 1970, Vol. 7651, p. 833-834.

13 Benson and Wallace, "Decreased Blood Pressure in Hypertensive Subjects," *CTS of the 45th Scientific Sessions,* 1972, Vol. 45.

14 F.M. Brown, W.S. Stewart, and J.T. Blodgett, "EEG Kappa Rhythms During TM," paper delivered to the Kentucky Academy of Sciences, Richmond, Kentucky, 1971.

15 J.P. Banquet, "EEG and Meditation," *Electroencephalography, Clinical Neurophysiology,* 1972, Vol. 33, pp. 449-50.

16 D.W. Orme-Johnson, "Autonomic Stability and TM," Proceedings: First Symposium on Science of Creative Intelligence, California State University at Humboldt, August, 1971.

17 S. Nidich, W. Seeman, and M. Seibert, "Influence of TM on State of Anxiety," *Journal of Consulting and Clinical Psychology* (In press, 1974).

18 L.A. Hjelle, "TM and Psychological Health," (Brockport: State University of New York).

19 J.M. Dechanet, *Christian Yoga* (New York: Harper Brothers, 1960), p. 231.

20 Ibid., p. 59.

21 Abraham Maslow, *Motivation and Personality* (New York: Harper Brothers, 1964).

CHAPTER 6

1 SIMS stands for Students' International Meditation Society, a name which was chiefly due to the fact that TM was originally most popular among college students. The organization has now dropped the S from its name.

2 K. Bladsdell, Ph.D. dissertation, University of California at Los Angeles, TM and Complex Perceptual Motor Tests, 1971.

3 A.I. Abrams, unpublished paper, University of California at Berkeley, "Paired Associate Learning and Recall," 1972.

4 R. Shaw and D. Kolb, unpublished paper, University of Texas at Austin, "One Point Reaction Time: Meditators versus Non-Meditators," 1971.

5 P.D. Ferguson and J. Gowan, "The Influence of TM on Anxiety, Depression, Aggression, Neuroticism, and Self-Actualization," *Journal of Humanistic Psychology* (in press, 1974).

6 Abraham Maslow, *Motivation and Personality* (New York: Harper Brothers, 1964).

7 W. Seeman, S. Nidich, and T. Banta, "Influence of TM on a Measure of Self-Actualization," *Journal of Counseling Psychology*, 1972, Vol. 19, p. 184.

8 Everett Shostrom, author of *Man the Manipulator*, has developed a research instrument for measuring the level of self-actualization.

9 David R. Frew, "TM and Productivity," *Proceedings; American Institute of Decision Sciences* (East Lansing: Michigan State University, 1973), p. 312.

10 David R. Frew, "TM and Productivity," *Academy of Management Journal*, June 1974, Vol. 17, No. 2, p. 362.

11 Significance testing was carried out between the hypothetical no-change scale value of 3.0 and the average position reported by meditators. Testing utilized a table of areas under the normal curve.

12 Frederick Hertzberg, *Work and the Nature of Man* (New York: World Publishing Company, 1966), p. 71.

13 W.W. Porter and E.E. Lawler have contributed to the general literature a large number of exciting articles dealing with motivation theory.

14 Significance tests were performed with both the Student's t-test and the Mann Whitney test in order to provide both parametric and nonparametric support for significance levels.

15 These statistics were presented by Dr. H. Bleilfield in a lecture given as a part of a symposium on TM and the Social Services, at Gannon College, Erie, Pa., during November 1974.

CHAPTER 8

1 Peter Drucker, *The Practice of Management* (New York: Harper, 1954).

2 Stephen Carroll and Henry Tosi, *Management by Objectives: Applications and Research* (New York: Macmillan, 1973).

3 Rex Hunt, "TA for Managers," *Management World*, 1973, p. 22.

4 A.H. Ismail and L.E. Trachtman, "Jogging the Imagination," *Psychology Today*, 1973, Vol. 17, p. 79.

5 For more information on the Benson approach see Herbert Benson, "Your Innate Asset for Combating Stress," *Harvard Business Review*, 1974, Vol. 52, p 49.

6 Pramahansa Yogananda, *Autobiography of a Yogi* (Los Angeles: Self-Realization Fellowship, 1946).

7 Franklin Loehm, *The Power of Prayer on Plants* (New York: Macmillan, 1972).

8 David Doner, Symposium, Connecticut Business and Industry Association, on November 22, 1974, at Connecticut General Life Insurance Company, Hartford, Connecticut.

CHAPTER 9

1 Warren Bennis, *Changing Organizations* (New York: McGraw-Hill, 1966), p. 196.

2 Ibid.

3 The "temporary-organization concept" is also borrowed from the works of Warren Bennis.

4 Paul Lawrence and Jay Lorsch, *Organization and Environment* (New York: Irwin, 1967).

5 "X" in this context refers to the theory of Douglas McGregor.

6 Herman Kahn and Anthony J. Wiener, *The Year 2000: A Framework for Speculation on the Next Thirty-three Years* (New York: Macmillan, 1967), p. 113.

7 Paul Erlick, *The Population Bomb* (New York: Ballentine Books, 1968).

8 This position has been described by Professor Robert Smith of Kent State University in a number of his papers and books.

9 Rensis Likert, *The Human Organization* (New York: McGraw-Hill, 1969).

10 Riva Poor, *Four Days, 40 Hours* (New York: Mentor Books, 1973).

11 Isaac Asimov, "The Falling Birthrate," from the column "Change" in *The American Way*, Nov. 1974, Vol. 7, No. 11, pp. 6-7.

Index